CW00421139

Published in 2010 by
Myrdle Court Press, London, UK

ISBN 978-0-9563539-2-4

Myrdle Court Press is an independent publishing
company that advances ideas
generated by emerging urbanists.

Unit 24 Myrdle Court, Myrdle Street, London E1 1HP
www.myrdlecourtpress.net

Designed by Karolin Schnoor
www.karolinschnoor.com

Printed and bound by Imprint Digital, Exeter, UK

Supported by

Estate

Fugitive Images

Fugitive Images is a platform for
artists collaborations to produce
work related to the ongoing changes
at Haggerston & Kingsland Estates.
It was founded in 2009 by Andrea
Luka Zimmerman, Lasse Johansson
and Tristan Fennell. For *Estate*
the collaboration consisted
of Paul Hallam in addition to the
founding members.

Table of Contents

DRIVE-BY CAREFULLY

fig.1

fig.2

Some Time in Utopia?

Andrea Luka Zimmerman
& Lasse Johansson

fig.3

Estate is an attempt to think through one of Britain's most significant utopian projects of the 20th century: public housing. It brings together a photograpic essay, a personal response to an experience of living on estates and two further essays that explore the historical and political context of estate life and reflect on the "archaeology of the recent past".

Estate sprang from our experience of the Haggerston West & Kingsland Estates in Hackney, East London, over the past two decades. We have lived in the area since 1991, and on Haggerston Estate itself since 1997. The idea for this book began to form as, from 2007, moves were made to demolish and reconstruct the estates. We wanted to record the changes this would inevitably bring. Though we interviewed many of the long– and short–term residents, the book is far from being an oral history or a definitive 'historical' account of the estates. It is a meditation on how history is forever rewritten but never easily told.

Rather than photographing its residents, we recorded the marks and impressions that people had made; and the photographic essay *In Wait* focuses on the curious and distinctive interventions in a 'regular' and to some extent standardised environment. We showed our photographs and transcripts of interviews to Paul Hallam. He drew on our correspondence and materials but brought his personal experiences of different estates to the fore, in part to reflect on the meaning of the word 'estate' itself. Victor Buchli brought his 'archaeological' approach to the material culture of estates that are so often condemned as failed if well–meaning social experiments. Finally, Cristina Cerulli considered the history and politics of public housing in the UK. Each of the book's parts reflect on and deepen the experience of the others.

It is our hope that together these different, at times contradictory, elements will constitute a work that suggests a mode of inquiry into the evocative, often derogative and contentious, term 'estate', here meaning public housing estates rather than a landed estate. Although many people have never

Andrea Luka Zimmerman, Lasse Johansson

set foot on a housing estate, let alone lived in one, most people seem to have strong opinions about them and their inhabitants. It strikes us, therefore, as particularly timely to publish this work now as we are perhaps about to lose forever public housing as it was championed and built during the 19th and 20th centuries.

Background

London County Council (LCC) began to build the Haggerston West & Kingsland Estates in 1928 and the last blocks on the Haggerston side were completed in 1948, while the Kingsland side was completed in 1953. The estates contained 480 flats in total, sizes ranged from 1 – 4 bedrooms. In those days a rather small 4–bedroom flat was expected to house a family of seven. For us today this may sound like unacceptable living conditions. However, when seen in relation to the current emphasis on building compact, high density, inner–city dwellings, it is worth asking what future generations will think when they look back and evaluate our current design strategies for the contemporary urban landscape.

When the original Haggerston Estate was completed it became known locally as the 'prestige blocks'. Many of the first residents to move into the estate came from so–called 'slum clearance programmes', a move not always as easy or as welcome for the participants as that term seems to suggest.[1] At the time there was assumed to be a strong connection between poverty, poor living conditions and moral deprivation. The expected add–on effect of the slum–clearance programmes was that the move into new, modern estates would improve not only the living conditions of the residents but also their moral character. In *Housing Problems,*[2] a seminal documentary from 1935 about slum clearance and the provision of new houses for the poor, the 'authoritative' voice–over for images showing former slum dwellers in their new homes proudly states: "When a public authority embarks on slum clearance work it must take people just as they are. It is however our experience, that if you provide people from the slums with decent homes they quickly respond to the improved conditions and keep their homes clean and tidy. In Stepney we are finding that the amount of interest which the people are taking in their new flats is advancing day by day."

The debate whether it is a combination of architecture and individual character flaws or wider systemic and structural inadequacies such as education and economic inequalities that create 'problem estates' is by no means over. Contemporary design policies, such as 'Secured by Design',[3] are still rooted in a belief that social problems on estates can be prevented simply by designing high–security residential areas. These measures are considered by landlords to sufficiently suppress criminal and anti–social behaviour. The question is not only whether such design in effect delivers more secure environments, but also more urgently whether it provides a social milieu suitable for human well–being.

Haggerston West & Kingsland Estates are located on opposite sides of Regent's Canal, which was built during the early 19th century to transport the raw materials needed by rapidly expanding industries. Due to changes in demand as well as in modes of transportation, it fell into disuse during the latter part of the 20th century. However, with the property boom beginning in the late 1990s, the canal found a new economic purpose: this time its role was symbolic and aesthetic rather than tangible and material. Regent's Canal with its scenic views offered plenty of development opportunities for real estate investors. As such, it is something like a gold vein running through the borough, increasingly dotted with exclusive warehouse conversions and luxury developments.

While this rapid transformation was going on in the nearby area, nothing much had changed on Haggerston West & Kingsland Estates since the early 1980s when they were transferred from the Greater London Council (GLC) to Hackney Council[4]. This turned out to be the first step in a drawn out process that would eventually end up with another transfer, which saw the ownership of the estates being transferred away from public ownership, by a vote of 71% of the residents on the estate, to L&Q housing association.

Before the GLC handed over the blocks to Hackney Council, a large part of the estate was emptied to allow for a partial refurbishment. Unlike the current regeneration project, where the residents are encouraged to return to the estate, in 1980 none of the residents were offered the opportunity to return once the refurbishment was completed. Thus the community was dispersed and the continuity of the estate life disrupted.

The transfer to Hackney Council also signalled the beginning of three decades of neglect. This led to the rapid exodus of key workers who, amongst others, had been allocated flats on the refurbished estate. The 1980s and 90s were characterised by transience. Tenants were given contracts with the promise of shortly being moved on to better and permanent arrangements. Some of these residents still live on the estate today. The past 30 years have seen many systemic failings, including the 'keys for cash' affair, where keys and tenancy agreements to flats on the estate were traded for individual profit. In the criminal investigation that followed, lengthy prison sentences were handed out to the guilty parties. During the 1990s at times as many as a third of the flats on the estate were squatted, many on a long–term basis, often but not always cohabiting peacefully with their council neighbours. Sadly the journey from 'prestige blocks' to 'sink estate' [5] was made complete in the early 90s when Haggerston Estate became known as the 'heroin capital of Europe'.[6]

During this period the management was characterised by a laissez–faire approach, leaving the estate in an increasingly desperate condition, though there was never a lack of promises of a brighter future. In fact, during the past 30 years, proposals to modernise the estate have come and gone with regularity, but none of them ever progressed beyond the planning stage. Perhaps partly because of this vacillation and uncertainty, major external and internal repairs were forever postponed.

Consequently, the housing blocks were gradually run down and left in a state of dilapidation.

For residents on the estate, like us, it created a sense of continuous suspension – a feeling of simultaneously being present and absent, never really knowing whether this would be our last winter spent in the cold and damp flats.

The present

In October 2007, all of this changed when the residents on the estate voted in favour of a regeneration package that would demolish the old blocks and build a new estate. Part of the estate has already been demolished and construction should soon commence.[7] All residents have been offered flats in the new development and will be temporarily re–housed during the demolition and construction phase.

It was the particular combination of the estate's history of neglect, decline and broken promises and its imminent regeneration that motivated us to embark on our estate project.[8] We were especially struck by what we perceived as an inherent ambiguity at the core of the regeneration process. On the one hand, there was a tangible sense of relief – finally everyone would have a decent flat to live in. On the other hand, we felt the presence of a strange kind of loss, which seemed difficult to grasp and quantify. In fact, the regeneration of the wider area carries with it an uneasy sense of inevitability. Nothing would stop Haggerston West & Kingsland Estates, and especially their recent past, from being buried deep beneath a flagship state–of–the–art regeneration project.[9]

We were intent on resisting the temptation to erase and forget, mainly because our own experience of the estate differs from the often clichéd narrative of 'trouble estates', which evokes a particular kind of social, economic and psychological place for which the only solution seems to be demolition. There's no denying it has been far from a perfect place over the years. But we must not forget it has also been a home for many

people, the place where some were born, spent their childhood, fell
and grew old. For us personally, it has been a home and sanctuary oft
amongst other things, an affordable place to live.

In equal measure, the process of regeneration itself intrigues us. How does it manage to manifest itself so forcefully, and quite often rather crudely, and yet remain somewhat elusive? What images and practices does it produce, distribute, omit and repress in order to transform the feel of an area in such a fundamental way?

In order to make sense of this process we turned to the French sociologist Pierre Bourdieu and his concept of habitus[10], which he defines as that which equips us with a sense of how to navigate our daily social world – the subtle learned behaviours handed down through patterns of conduct by our social group, its history, culture, languages and norms. Bourdieu describes the feeling of being "at home in one's world" as follows: "When habitus encounters a social world of which it is the product, it finds itself 'as a fish in water', it does not feel the weight of the water and takes the world about itself for granted."[11] The regeneration of our area seemed to us to do something similar but in reverse. By changing the temperature of the area, some groups and individuals would begin to feel the weight of the water around them, whereas others would be accommodated, take it for granted and feel like fish in its waters.

As photographers, we were interested to look at how habitus might have manifested or engraved itself in the material culture of the multiple domestic environments on the estate – be they recently vacated flats due to re–housing or still lived–in homes. However, the unruly social world of human beings once again proved itself resistant to highly specified, conceptual abstractions such as habitus. What we found on the estate was of course not a clearly definable and uniform habitus able to accurately represent the entire community. Rather we found something more akin to a complex network of coexisting social worlds, reflecting the varied lifestyles and cultural backgrounds of people on the estate.

Just as these social worlds do not exist in isolation from each other on the estate, neither can they be separated from the surrounding area. On the contrary, they are further positioned and defined by such an extended context. Therefore we decided to momentarily step out of the estate in order to look at how it is described and defined by the ongoing regeneration of the surrounding area. We explored the production of visual materials used to promote the up–and–coming area and found an almost complete absence of the local population that has been living in the area for decades or even generations.[12] They are simply not addressed. In such promotional material there are no traces of their rich and diverse lifestyles, their values and tastes. On the contrary, these communities are often stigmatised by the process leading up to an area becoming ripe for regeneration, which regularly includes landlords and/or management agencies 'marking' estates for redevelopment by letting them become run–down. It is a process that can go on for years, at times even decades, and often the act of 'marking' becomes quite aggressive. This is what happened at Haggerston West & Kingsland Estates. Without any prior warning or consultation with residents, five months *before* the stock transfer vote that was to decide the future of the estate, Hackney Homes[13] fitted bright orange boards over the windows of all the empty flats.[14] This effectively set the estate apart from its surroundings, marking it abject. Overnight the estate became an object of curiosity and a considerable photo opportunity for passers–by on the canal.

Undeniably, there are actors in the regeneration process who are driven by a genuine sense of conviction and commitment to provide people with a better and affordable place to live. But equally, regeneration is nested in a financial network that depends on and requires profit margins insuring that investments will yield dividends. During the 12 years of economic growth preceding the 2008 banking crisis and global financial downturn, Haggerston West & Kingsland Estates were left adrift, seemingly unaffected by the inflated housing market and the prosperous economy.

It was not until towards the end of this era of boom economy and with the help of a winning Olympic bid and local improvements in infrastructure, such as the extension of the East London Line, that Haggerston West & Kingsland Estates started to become a viable option for regeneration. The development will carry no loss of social housing but, in order to help finance the project, it will contain a doubling in density due to additional private and shared ownership flats.[15]

Thatcherite economics, eagerly continued and fulfilled by New Labour, championed the idea of a trickle–down effect, which claimed that the creation of wealth in an area would trickle down and benefit its poorer parts. The problem with this is two–fold. First, it embodies a logic of 'aspiration', where one should continually desire to have 'more'. Second, it could also be argued that when luxury developments, designer shops, artisan bakeries, high–end food markets etc., begin to crop up in a poor area there is an additional side–effect, which is that these opposites – rich and poor – tend to amplify each other and, rather than any trickle–down, they even further articulate the vast socio–economic difference that exists between them.

According to Wilkinson and Pickett in *The Spirit Level*, this is a situation not to be taken lightly.[16] On the contrary, they argue that the most corrosive element in a society, which breeds the worst social ills such as high crime rates and poor health, is inequality in all its various manifestations. They also argue that when a society has achieved a certain level of wealth greater happiness and well–being are no longer dependent on further increases and accumulation of more wealth. Instead, at this level of development, to further increase the welfare of a society, the focus should be on issues of equality, such as making sure all citizens are seen and treated as worthy and valued members of that society. This appears to indicate that at a certain level of economic development the struggle for equality becomes a symbolic one concerned with determining and defining values rather than further increases in material wealth. In other words, equality becomes a question of what is championed and what is discarded, and how such classifications are determined and by whom.

'Pepper–potting' is the name given to the mix often found on new housing developments that includes social housing tenants and shared ownership schemes as well as for sale properties. It means social tenants live side–by–side with homeowners and tenants renting privately. This is the kind of mix that most accurately represents the socio–economic mix of the society at large. However, pepper–potting is not popular amongst estate agents, property speculators and buyers as there is a fear that the future selling of flats may be compromised due to the proximity to the social tenants. As a consequence, mixed developments regularly have separate entrances and stairwells for social tenants and private tenants. Equally, the private flats have often catered for the buy–to–let market. This had the opposite effect to the original intention with pepper–potting, which was to avoid creating pockets of high concentration of benefit dependency and social deprivation. According to the trickle–down philosophy, such a mixture of rich and poor would encourage and inspire the less wealthy. However, as these properties turned into a good investment for property speculators on the buy–to–let market, they became the most transient part of communities, turning over private tenants at a much higher rate than the adjacent social–housing flats. Thus they did not provide the stability to the community that was initially intended.

Estate is about these complex processes and politics of place making, how places are remembered as well as how they are forgotten. We are animated by the desire to explore a place that it would be much easier to forget. Through the book's form, we seek to question what memories are considered 'worthy' of being remembered, what images and narratives 'deserve' a place in history, and what will end up on the cutting–room floor.

We are not interested in simply uncovering a past world from the safe distance of the present, which we believe often caters for a nostalgic engagement with the archive, depicting for example a lost world where children played innocently in the early 1930s' estate courtyard, a place where "you could always leave your door unlocked", or the transformation of those playgrounds into air–raid shelters during World War II.

Our interest is rather in how to remember and make sense of the last 30 years of decline at the estate, when it became known as a 'sink estate'. Yes, there is ample evidence of vulnerability, illness and neglect. But there is also ingenuity, a sense of play, resilience and humour. What we found particularly striking, in this economic milieu of small means, were the interventions and innovations that eloquently displayed a refusal to resign or simply accept the hand that had been dealt.

Sadly developers, housing managers, authorities and architects often appear to notice and focus mainly on the problems they find or perhaps predict they will encounter. There is an impression that such agents have long fixed their perception of certain communities as unruly, and therefore concluded that they are at least in part the source of their own demise. This makes it appear as if it is the community that is in need of reform. This failure to recognise the resources of a community appears to us as indicative of how poverty is institutionalised and systemic. It also suggests that poverty is inseparable from how we see and therefore experience and form opinions about each other. In addition it raises questions about how we imagine progress.

The question about what the future might bring to the estate is perhaps more present today than anytime during the 30 years of decline. Curiously, in this period of transition, there has been an openness. Perched precariously somewhere in between the recent past and the imminent future, the ambiguity of this moment is powerfully played out against the backdrop of the ongoing demolition of the estate. The partially occupied Samuel House is the last block still standing on the Haggerston West side of the estates, with about two years to go before it is demolished as part of Phase II. In what is the dying moment of a particular era in public housing, Samuel House is experiencing what is best described as a revival. With no future to tend or be maintained for, there is a great sense of freedom on what remains of the estate. Gradually it is being transformed, even customised by the residents. With the introduction of picnic tables, BBQ facilities and a table–tennis table, the courtyard has been turned into the meeting place it was presumably originally designed to be. Perhaps it is possible to read the current moment of openness at Haggerston West & Kingsland Estates as a utopian echo of an abandoned public housing ideal.

This moment of suspension has allowed for an injection of community engagement, which further foregrounds the question of what the future might bring. The new estate will arrive with a package of regulations, put in place to control the management and security of the estate.[17] The question is: how far will these regulations go and what impact will they have on the community life of the estate?

There are tendencies indicating that housing management and building design are increasingly modelled on health and safety regulations, as articulated in design ideals and policies such as 'defensible space' [18] and 'Secured by Design' [19]. These ideas have of late engraved themselves on the surface of the urban landscape through an increasing number of gated community type of developments, be they social housing or luxury developments for more affluent citizens. This trend in turn is influenced by the insurance industry through setting the rate of premiums charged to insure the buildings in accordance with how well a new development conforms to such security ideals. This relationship creates a problematic link between the insurance industry and the built environment. In *Ground Control,* Anna Minton emphasises that "defensible space and high levels of security are built into virtually all new housing to attract lower insurance premiums, creating a virtuous circle for developers, who charge a premium for it".[20]

The future?

With due respect to security and economic benefit, the key question is whether this is the best way to create the platform for community life to develop? Minton argues that with the increasing fixation on security, which is achieved by locking out, with the help of gates and CCTV cameras, all external and unwanted elements, we are running the risk of creating a false sense of security by excluding the unexpected. It creates a sense that everyone not belonging to the environment is a potential danger in need of surveillance. "By retreating into safe havens, which substitute physical security and complex technological systems to meet emotional needs, this way of living is in danger not only of dividing the landscape but of stymieing people's emotional lives in the process, by creating the false illusion that life is 'psychologically snug' (Giddens) and perfectly safe. When forced to venture out of these environments, the danger is that people are far less able to cope with the ordinary risks that are part of healthy life than they were before."[21]

'Defensible' housing? Or housing that might be more open, less 'safe'? We hope that this book contributes in some way to an already complex debate; that it not only evokes memories, but also provokes thoughts on a future where exclusivity and exclusion should surely be indefensible.

1. See text by P. Hallam on page 82.
2. *Housing Problems*, directed by Arthur Elton & Edgar Anesty, produced by the British Commercial Gas Association, London, 1935.
3. See essay by C. Cerulli on page 117.
4. London County Council (LCC) was replaced in 1965 by the Greater London Council (GLC) which in turn was dismantled in 1986 by the Conservative government.
5. See essay by C. Cerulli on page 117.
6. In response to this label, a local film collective made the film *Haggerston is not just Heroin.*
7. See image on page 140.
8. Starting in the autumn of 2007, just after the transfer vote, we decided to begin working as artists on the estate. Both Hackney Council and L&Q gave us access to photograph the empty flats as people moved out and the estate was gradually emptied of people. As we continued to document the estate we got to know our neighbours better and began filming with them, a work that is still continuing. In 2009, together with our fellow residents, we installed a public artwork called *i am here* (www.iamhere.org.uk) on the facade of Samuel House. The installation replaced all the orange boards on the block with large-scale portraits of current residents and those who had recently moved out. All along we kept documenting the

interiors of empty flats and gradually we began to photograph those flats that were still lived in.

9. The Haggerston West & Kingsland development in many ways represents the current state-of-the-art social housing project with a priority given to high-density living, security and mixed tenure. According to PRP, the architects responsible for the design of the blocks, the development is: "A significant London estate creating high-density living. Emphasis has been given in designing an individual feeling estate with a safe and secure environment for residents including improved car parking and open spaces for community living." (http://www.prparchitects.co.uk/our-sectors/urban-regeneration/haggerston.html)The estate will have a mixed tenure consisting of socially rented flats and affordable for-sale units as well as private units. No loss of social housing will occur and all the current residents have been have been promised a return to the new development.
10. See for example, Pierre Bourdieu, *The Field of Cultural Production* (New York: Columbia University Press, 1993).
11. Pierre Bourdieu and Loic Wacquant, *An Invitation to Reflexive Sociology* (London & Chicago: Polity Press, University of Chicago Press, 1992) p. 12.
12. For example: 'Play the regeneration game' in *Homes & Property*, 24 May 2010, text materials and images found on billboards and in brochures in the local area produced by estate agents to promote the sales of newly built flats. The billboards show actors representing the imagined future tenants: professionals in crisp and clean, designer flats.
13. "Hackney Homes was launched in April 2006 and is responsible for managing council homes in Hackney. This includes managing council housing, collecting council housing rental, repairing and maintaining council homes" (Hackney Homes, website, 2010).
14. See image on p.03
15. The new development will consist of 761 new homes, 418 affordable, of which 248 will be for rent and 343 will be private. All the 'affordable' housing will be between 10–15% larger than the Parker Morris standard.
16. Richard Wilkinson and Kate Pickettand, *The Spirit Level: Why More Equal Societies Almost Always Do Better* (London: Penguin, 2010).
17. For example, the new estate will have CCTV cameras. The previously open access estate, with its communal green space accessible to residents and public alike, will be divided into several city blocks with internal courtyards accessible only to the residents in each block. In effect this will turn a currently continuous residential space into independent units/blocks. How this will affect the sense of being part of one community only the future will tell.
18. See Oscar Newman, *Creating Defensible Space*, pdf downloadable, for a fee, at:http://www.defensiblespace.com/start.htm.
19. See http://www.securedbydesign.com/.
20. Anna Minton, *Ground Control* (London: Penguin, 2009) p. 74.
21. *Ibid.*, Minton (2009) p. 81.

In Wait

Fugitive Images

Stamp Album
Cover Album

fig.4

fig.5

fig.6

fig.7

fig.8

fig.9

fig.10

SR

Hackney Gazette

FOUNDED 1864

FRIDAY, MAY 9, 1975

No. 15,176

AND NORTH LONDON ADVERTISER

5p.

TENANTS' FEARS CONFIRMED

Face-lift plans for estates are shelved

HOXTO

FOR T

EIGHT

SCHOOLMATES o[f] part in today's fu[neral] old who died in [...] his first holiday [...] service was arrang[ed] adjoining the pr[...] remembered as a l[...]

Since the tragedy [...] day, messages of sy[mpathy] have been pouring i[n] Crondall Court,

fig.11

fig.12

fig.13

fig.14

fig.15

fig.16

RCA
Stereo 8
ELVIS PRESLEY
Rock'n'Roll
1
2
3
4
BARRY WHITE
CAN'T GET ENOUGH

fig.17

fig.18

fig.19

fig.20

fig.21

fig.22

fig.23

fig.24

fig.25

fig.26

fig.27

fig.28

fig.29

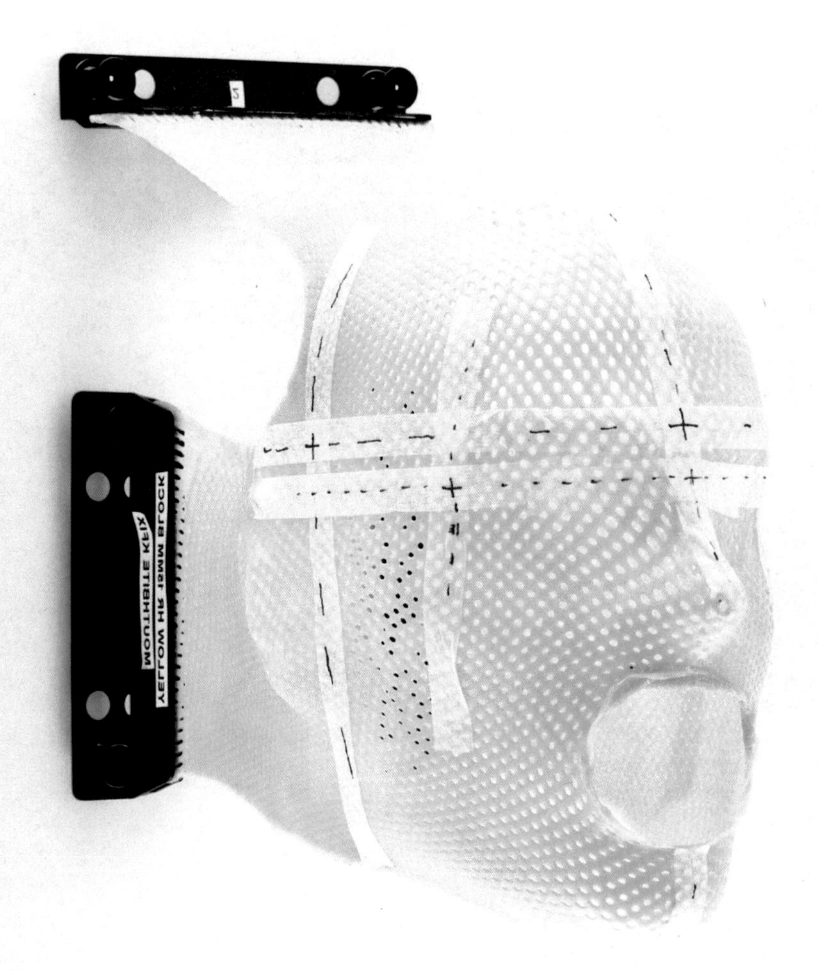

fig.30

fig.31

fig.32

fig.33

fig.34

fig.35

fig.36

fig.37

fig.38

MANCHESTER UNITED
2006/07
MANUTD.COM
grand theft auto
Vice City Stories

fig.39

fig.40

fig.41

fig.42

fig.43

fig.44

fig.45

fig.46

X9 FLINTS
RONSON
FIREBRONZE
Premium Quality
FLINTS
X9 FLINTS

fig.47

fig.48

fig.49

fig.50

HAGGERSTON 1940

We were asked to write something about old Haggerston. I thought it would be a good idea to relate how the shopping area used to be. I asked my niece Rose Phillips for her help and her memory is fantastic.

<u>The Year 1940</u>

Black Bull Public House
A Barbers
Langs - Drapers
Hanchards - Sweet Shop
Salmons - Wet Fish Shop
Wings - Florists
A Laundry which did "Best" as well as what was called "Bag Wash"
Bob's Fish Shop
Moles - Grocers
Paddon's - Butchers
Len's - Hairdressers
A Chemist
Bob Lincoln's Cafe
Maxwell - Bag Wash Laundry
Yellands - General Store
Norman's - Bakers
Sawyer's - Butchers
French - Green grocers
Owen's - Dairy
Lawrence - Grocers
Mann Crossman Public House
'Italian' Mary's Cafe
A Coal Shop which not only sold coal but also bought rags for a few pence
A Bike shop - which sold second hand bikes and did repairs
A Pawnshop
Lant & Marshall - Clothing
Dolly's - Bakers (known as Dolly's but she wasn't the owner).
Howards - Newsagent
Haggerston Mission
Another laundry
Another newsagent
The Working Men's Club
Duke of Sussex Public House

It doesn't seem possible that there were so many shops in this area considering it was quite a poor district.

All Saints Church Hall played an important part in the life of Haggerston, where activities of all kinds took place every day and evening. There were clubs, dancing lessons, exercise classes, Brownies, Cubs, Girl Guides and Rangers and Scouts, plus parties and weddings, and of course religious instruction and prayer groups.

fig.51

11pm

TESCO
£2
Meal Deal
Buy 1 Get 1 FREE
Pepsi & Pepsi Max
£1
Kellogg's Variety
£1
Kit Kat

fig.52

Index

1. "Please drive by Carefully in our village", by Banksy, on the old Haggerston bridge, which was demolished and rebuilt to make way for the East London line extension, 2004, photo by Nick Strauss.
2. The new face of the area, 2010.
3. Orange Boards to cover void units were installed on the façade of Haggerston Estate in April 2007, five months before the transfer vote to decide the future of the estate. Also, see Gerard Johnson's Tony, 2009, sporting the orange boards; tag line: "a thriller centred on a serial killer in a rundown London suburb". To catch a glimpse of the estate without the orange boards watch Mike Leigh's Meantime, 1983,starring Tim Roth and Gary Oldman, a movie about crumbling Britain during the Thatcher years.
4. After a peak in burglaries in the early 1990s many flats on the estate had metal bars fitted across windows and iron gates installed. The gates are used to secure the low–quality front doors, some of which could easily be kicked in. During the hot summer months, the gates allow for wide open doors and windows, even during the night.
5. The aquarium still had water and some remains of plastic plants in it but no fish. The tiled area was where the old fireplace used to be, a gas heater installed in its place. Some of the older flats had large–scale fireplaces for cooking in and their outline can still be seen on the dented plaster in the walls, usually also sporting a gas heater in its stead. We always wondered what happened to the now so sought after iron casings and who uses them now, or whether they were melted into something else. One of the residents had picked up an enormous fireplace, salvaged from the Bank of Scotland backyard

when its City of London headquarters were modernised. She was a cleaning–staff supervisor at the bank.

6. Many of the flats had items of clothing left behind. Not on the floor or in piles, but still hanging, in wardrobes, on coat hangers. And usually, a certain amount of toiletries.

7. There was no wardrobe in this flat, just two long clotheslines spanning across the room. Apart from the boxes and hangers, the flat was empty.

8. Curiously in quite a few of the flats we found abandoned pairs of crutches. There was nothing in this flat apart from the St George's Cross, which was painted over a clothes hook that seemed to be in the way, and these crutches, which presumably were no longer needed.

9. This oil burner is a relic from the past; we found several on this estate. Beautiful as they are, they are usually not fondly remembered as they smoked a lot and produced soot.

10. Another example of a previous fireplace that had been turned into a gas heater. Instead of tiles, the mantelpiece is wood. The contents of the flat had been packed up in preparation for the temporary re–housing. All the shelves had been removed. The light washing through the window against the wall made the room look like it belonged to a Victorian house.

11. Hackney Gazette cover, 9 May 1975, No. 15176. Only two years previously, residents had gone on rent strike to enforce modernisations, as reported on Hackney Gazette cover, 30 January 1973, No. 14950.

12. A desk full of paint and speckles of paint all around on the floor. Inside the drawer, tubes of paint and a few used brushes.

13. A bag made by a men's wear fashion designer who has lived on the estate most of his life. Sm.ART came to the UK when he was 6 years old and is inspired by fabrics that explore migration politics as well as exclusive designs. "In 1983, more than a million Ghanaians were expelled from Nigeria. In their rush to flee the country, these refugees turned cheap bags of woven plastic into makeshift luggage. These bags are now commonly referred to in Nigeria as well as over here amongst African communities as a 'Ghana must go'."

14. This flat was so mouldy that the air was hard to breathe. We were told the windows had to be kept open throughout the winter to alleviate some of the problems associated with the dampness. This part of the estate, which was the first to be demolished, had a major roof leak that had been ignored long enough to cause irreversible damage to dwellings. The only room where mould was not growing visibly along the walls was the living room.

15. In this flat, a beauty that belonged to a previous era. Everything seemed original, from the built–in Electrolux fridge to the fitted cupboards, which were a better quality than anything that came after the flats were modernised in the 1980s. It was as if this flat had escaped all attempts to modernise it. It had only been occupied by one resident, who lived there all her life, and when she moved to an old people's home the flat was bricked up and has since been demolished.

16. Quite a few of the flats contained polystyrene ceiling tiles, which were a popular decorative element in the 1980s. The material was inexpensive, lightweight and could easily be moulded to different designs. Most of these 'styro ceiling tiles' were made to look as though they were plaster, copper or aluminium, giving an 'antique' look. The tiles were highly inflammable, especially when painted. The burning substance turned to a liquid lethal rain that would drip, still in flames, onto anything and anybody underneath, thus spreading the fire quickly. In the late 1980s, the UK Public Information Department produced a film advising viewers on the risk of the tiles. However, once installed, the tiles were difficult toremove and many still remained on Haggerston West & Kingsland Estate.

17. Because people had aged with their flats, their technology often outlived its market use. This fully working 8–track machine with large selection of discs was used even after cassettes were in fashion. A cassette to 8–track adaptor tape where a smaller cassette could be inserted into the larger tape case allowed their music taste to evolve unhindered.
18. Over the years the 'anti graffiti' teams worked hard on denying any public markings on stairwells or walls. Councils deem such markings anti social, excesses of public expression that undermine order and need curtailing. We found this marking particularly touching, a clear display of love to a granddad. In what might have been an attempt to preserve the lighter fluid, the marker took one 'd' out of 'granddad'.
19. Many beds were left behind. This seems to indicate, more than anything else, that at least some of these were furnished lets, which would include housing associations subletting flats from the council and providing furnished temporary accommodation for its residents.
20. This flat, entirely empty, apart from a set of hair rollers.
21. This wall was panelled above another fireplace converted to gas heater and was the main focus of the living room with its Arsenal poster, brasses, paintings and other decorations. The room was still festooned for Christmas in a flat that belonged to one of the first residents to leave the block. It is now demolished.
22. Eclectic bedroom interior.
23. Many times we came across flats that had been carefully cleaned, often even hoovered, before being handed over to the builders waiting to brick up the doors and windows to wait for demolition.
24. During the 1990s, cars were frequently fly–tipped in and around the estate and often set alight by bored youth. As we write this, in July 2010, this tradition has again returned to the estate with two cars set alight in the past month.

25. Improvised shoe divider inside wardrobe.

26. A collection of fine red glassware built up during a lifetime. Most of the items were purchased from Harrods and only a small fraction of them were displayed in the living–room cabinet. The owner of the collection moved to the estate from Hoxton in a slum–clearance programme. At the age of 90, she has just moved to Essex to live close to her granddaughter.

27. As the estate has an open entrance, metal gates help prevent things being stolen from the landings. The flats are very small and over the years fridges, washing machines, bikes and cupboards have been moved out to the landing to make more space inside. Like many people on Haggerston Estate we could never fit our fridge in the kitchen because it was too small. We had to keep it in the living room until our heater was exchanged and the old water tank was removed from the kitchen area. Most people put plants and chairs on the landing to make it more homely and used it like a balcony.

28. The amount of colour people had in their flats was astonishing. The standard '60 minute turnover' type decorating simply does not apply here and we wonder if it does apply at all, apart from in hotels, show flats or TV shows.

29. 'Bread Jesus' was made in the home of a practising Catholic. The inspiration for the artwork came while she was eating a piece of baguette and an image of Jesus appeared to her in one of the pieces of bread lying on the plate. She dried the bread and painted it with nail varnish.

30. Specially moulded facemask used during radio therapy treatment to line up the exact area in need of treatment.

31. The bathrooms and kitchens on the estate are very small and lack sufficient shelf and surface space.

32. Residents in several flats used discarded wardrobes as cabinets and ceiling storage. The wardrobe as kitchen cupboard was particularly interesting as a simple idea that could easily have been a really expensive designer shop item. The door had a holding mechanism, which meant it didn't just fall shut.

33. We were particularly drawn to small adaptations, ingenious alterations and re–use of things in new and different ways. This is exemplified here by this safety contraption. We had never seen a door chain used in this way before, tried it, and found it was really quite effective to keep a cat out of the bedroom.

34. We have an informal recycling scheme going on at the estate, which means that most of our furniture has at some point belonged to someone else, and in turn our discarded furniture has ended up in other homes. When someone puts furniture downstairs and it is in good condition it usually finds a home within minutes. We frequently saw chairs and bits we once used in other flats and here part of our discarded futon base had found a new use as a plug board in a neighbouring flat.

35. Nearly every flat we photographed had taped up the air vents in response to the draughts and consequently very cold conditions, especially during the winter months.

36. Bed board and a taped–up air vent with several layers of tape stuck on to hold the closure in place.

37. Improvised antenna holder.

38. The pipes are hidden behind plywood panels and much space goes to waste in the small flats. In order to make use of this wasted space a hole has been cut into the plywood to make a storage alcove for the mop. Many of the flats had severe mould due to dampness; this shower curtain was used to cover up a mouldy wall.

39. A room defying the description 'standard white'.

40. This flat shouted with vibrant colours.

41. Signs of someone slipping beneath the layers of the supposedly protective social services of a welfare state. It worried us as we saw this happen to residents we got to know personally, whose lives were not lived in happy ways or happy conditions. A care system, which needs skills to navigate and persistence to break through, does not necessarily provide for fiercely proud, independent but physically ill individuals. Their fear that their desire to live 'at home', not 'in a home', would not be valued if they were to involve social services kept them isolated and uncared for. This flat had only recently been vacated.

42. Halloween mask next to bed.

43. Toothache remedy in what appeared to have been a suddenly abandoned flat. Everything was seemingly left in place, looking as if everyday life could continue just as suddenly as it had been stopped in its track.

44. The shoes seemed as if someone had just slipped them off. There was a red hospital chair in the background and a chestnut wardrobe in the corner, full of clothes. With everything still inside, the flat was waiting for the bulldozers.

45. Ornaments on a gas heater installed where the fireplace would have been in the past.

46. B&W television, found in empty flat. As soon as we plugged it in our lights flittered and shortly after –this picture was taken the TV wiring blew our electricity out.

47. Flints for lighters, a common sight in the days before 'disposables'. "Friends" newsagent, situated on Haggerston Estate, is the only corner shop within a mile's radius where these flints are still sold.

48. Gas pipe stumps, empty flat. As metal prices skyrocketed in 2007, the poorly bricked–up, void units on the estate were easily broken into and pipes stolen. When water pipes were removed the surrounding flats often flooded due to the oversight of the authorities to turn off the water supply to the void units.

49. Bricked–up outside landing, a frequent feature on the estate in an attempt to prevent illegal entry to vacated flats and also to stop the flooding which was a side effect of copper pipes being stolen. This wall was painted and decorated with three pictures, which lasted about two months before they disappeared.

50. Omlette'n chips in a tin, found in empty flat.

51. Haggerston 1940, an inventory of the shops along Haggerston Road, compiled by an elderly lady who lived in the neighbourhood all her life.

52. Tesco Express, one of increasingly many within walking distance of Haggerston West & Kingsland Estate, 2010, photo by Fugitive Images.

53. Booth Map, courtesy of the Booth Collection, LSE Archives, London School of Economics and Political Science, 10 Portugal Street, WC2A2HD. Haggerston West comprises the area mainly in blue, with three black lines. All Saints is at the top of the estate, and the Black line at the bottom is where Samuel House now stands [2010].

54. Haggerston Estate being partially demolished, phase 1, 2010, photo by Ruth–Marie Tunkara.

55. PRP Architects model of the planned new estate, L&Q offices, 2008, photo by Fugitive Images.

THE STREETS A

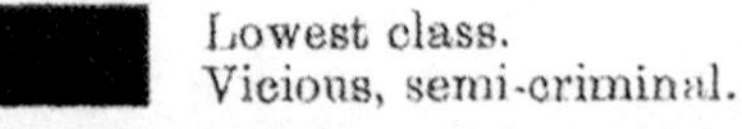

Lowest class.
Vicious, semi-criminal.

Very poor, casual.
Chronic want.

fig.53

URED ACCORDING TO THE GENERAL CONDITION OF THE INHABITA

s. to 21s. a week
oderate family.

Mixed. Some comfortable,
others poor.

Fairly comforta
Good ordinary e

Estate

Paul Hallam

I was born in Garden Road, Mansfield, though there was little sign of a garden. There was a rough back yard and alleyway. If I mention the tin bath, the outside lavatory, there's the risk of a "humble origin" northern English nostalgia.

Even though I have stayed there from time to time, I have never been an official resident, never been moved "onto" or "off" the Haggerston Estate.

True, all of my letters, diaries, photographs and personal notes are in a flat there, in a large metal trunk, and in a few old cases. I have never before been separated from them for more than a month or two. The materials perhaps for an autobiography I might one day get around to writing.

Not everything on an estate belongs to its current residents. There are traces of those who briefly stayed or simply passed through. Visitors, friends, ex-lovers, the dead.

Occasionally I wake, thinking of one part or another of my particular trunk, and my changing relation to its contents, now that it is not with me to be looked at, not that I ever looked into it much when it was closer to hand.

I have never stayed in Haggerston long enough to write a "walk piece" or a "view from the window"; never been there long enough to catch a sense of its ordinary daylight, its everyday. Perhaps, if I try to wander the estate through the resident accounts, mostly second–hand, mostly sent to me by the photographers, sometimes with notes and comments, with responses to my questions about the estate.

Lots of kids swam in the canal,
but then in the late 80s such swimming was made illegal, for health and safety.

He said there was a big tree next to the estate; that it needed four people to hug it. The tree fell in the big storm during the 1980s and crashed a newly built house, on Stonebridge Estate opposite to Haggerston.

With the surge in Chinese demand for metal in 2007/2008 the price of scrap metal skyrocketed. Soon the interest in the bricked–up flats, or rather the metal left in them, increased significantly. Since Hackney Council had used only the cheapest of bricks it was not much of an effort to break into the empty flats and collect the desired pipes and water tanks. The only slight side–effect was the flooding of neighbouring flats.

Apparently, some 300 years ago, there were tobacco processing plants here.

There used to be patrol men in vans on the estate with yellow lights on top making sure everyone was ok ... hmmm?

Helios man, 1600s, lived across the canal, and all sorts of discoveries were made here in Haggerston, some famous scientists etc.

There's another estate in Westminster, next to the Houses of Parliament, called the Dolphin Estate, which is similar to this one here, but Princess Anne has a flat there and they have regular tea parties, a posh version of this one.

Our Nan and Granddad had moved into number 10, Lowther House, about six months before us. The estate was still being built. Grandfather had gassed himself along with his little dog, Dinah. They'd come from a place where he had a donkey, pony, a goose, chickens and grew veg. to a one bedroom flat, it must have been hard to take.

We were moved because of slum clearance from a small house in Hockley Street off Morning Lane Hackney, our street, and the adjoining Woolpack Place and Ribstone Street. Most old neighbours were hardworking street traders but of course there were also quite a few bad eggs. The council decided to split the people up and they were put onto different estates. Our Mum loved the flat as soon as she walked in and saw the sun blasting through the bay windows.

Before we moved in, I remember all the bedding had to be fumigated (not just ours by the way, everyone's). Mother was thrilled to have a bathroom, which had a gas geyser that had to be lit with a match. Not having experienced such a thing before, the gas was turned on before having lit the match, and whoosh a small explosion, known as a blow back. Frightened the life out of our Mum but turned out to be a regular occurrence with a lot of the tenants. We'd hear these small bangs mostly on a Sunday morning, the once a week bath time.

We knew all the neighbours, the lady who lent money out was Mrs Wilson, she lived in the top flat, she charged a small interest on what she lent.

A couple of years ago while doing a crossword I noticed that the names of the flats were all related to Samuel Richardson's books. Maybe someone on the council was a fan?

I might have enjoyed hearing the stories, but once written down these sometimes bleak but often funny and moving memories make me uncomfortable.

The feeling that oral stories are best kept oral.

I cannot believe I started this with "I was born". The risk of a humble origin nostalgia, I am aware of it, but cannot resist the tin bath mention.

It never felt humble. Nor did anyone in my family ever strike me as humble.

Can an estate consist of just a few roads, some old stone Victorian houses at the top of the road, looking down on the more recent redbrick terraces? Is an estate always a closed–off area, with the pleasures and restrictions perhaps of a self–contained island? They seem to be somewhere you arrive at, often with some difficulty, they are often vast and complex, with an array of entrances and exits, marked with special wood and metal boards, these are meant to help you to deal with the wealth of house and block names.

I still like to arrive, to find my way, without recourse to a mobile phone. Any difficulties finding the place are often compounded by these boards. You are a stranger, somewhat anxiously negotiating the terrain that the residents so take for granted.

Admit it, those stairwells can be scary. Garden Road was not like that, just down the road, the town centre, just around the corner the Mansfield Railway Station.

Mansfield, a plain name, was very much inland. I could and did steal leaflets from the local train station; they were in pale colours and offered daytrips to the exotic sounding seaside of Bridlington, Cleethorpes, Mablethorpe, Skegness. At the time I had no way of knowing that such grand place names would be smiled at; to others, the names merely evoked saucy postcards, candyfloss and "kiss me quick" hats. I treasured the timetables and stored and arranged them in an old lilac–painted wooden sideboard that had been relegated or rather uplifted to the attic. Until one day the massive stash was discovered and the childhood collection was quickly curtailed.

We moved to a modern house, Bonington Road on Ladybrook Estate, no scary coal cellar or dark attic, just a loft with an insulation tank. There was a garden at the front, the back and even one at the side. Though the road was a steep climb from the nearest bus stop, the view over the town was worth it. A council house, but semi–detached with rough stretches to hide, play and kick around on. Ladybrook stretched for miles, a collection of unconnected streets, it felt more like a loose association of rival estates within the estate.

A third move, nearer to the pit and with an extra bedroom, was to a Coal Board estate, known as a tough one. Many miners from Newcastle and Scotland had moved down there, as their collieries were one by one shut down. Kelvin Close, Garibaldi Estate. Its rhythms were dictated by the days, "afters", nights, the shifts of the men who worked down the mines. Something of the Quaker estate about it, in as much as it kept the workers together, in one place. It never struck me as at all odd that an estate should revolve round a single industry, though the women might have jobs outside of it, full or part–time in factories or in shops. It didn't cross my mind that this might be socially somewhat restricting. I don't recall ever seeing a black or an Asian face on the estate. But in Mansfield, by Titchfield Park, there were large "extended" families of "Poles" who ate a different kind of food, they played card games a lot and had a social club with erratic and equally extended opening hours. I knew that, I had a friend, Josef Poniatowski, at school. He took me home to meet his family; it seemed larger than any family could possibly be.

The "Polacks" got some teasing as did the other Catholics, but they were fortunate in being excused school "assembly", as was the one Jewish boy. Otherwise the Polish seemed quite normal. Garibaldi's Scots and Geordies were much more the "foreigners", they seemed wilder, and their accents took a lot more getting used to. Anyway, soon enough everyone was, and seemed to be speaking "Mansfield".

On Garibaldi there was little of the care or ingenuity of the Quaker concept of the workers' estate. No hall, no centre, not even a pub. There was a row of shops that served it. Late at night it could feel quite forbidding, Mods and Rockers ("Grebos") revved and roved around it. For a year or two, I had no idea who or what Garibaldi was, apart from a biscuit, no idea why the estate was thus named. It was just Garibaldi or "Gara", you "lived up Gara", the estate with a "reputation".

There were call boxes on the corner, from which you might, should they be working, call out or even receive calls if you were prepared to wait long enough. You might walk past them sometimes and hear the phone ring; and you could answer it and hear the disappointment of someone hoping that someone else was waiting to take the arranged time call. You might even be asked to take a message to a resident just across the road.

I invariably answered if I heard the phone ringing, in search of a curious random adventure.

I could go out from Garibaldi, the estate of my adolescence to a wood, or take a bus to visit a country estate, at that time Nottinghamshire and Derbyshire "country piles" were slowly opening to an eager public; though their owners might have some parts firmly fenced off with clear "Not Open to the Public" signs. Clumber Park, Hardwick Hall and Byron's Newstead Abbey. On another "day out", I might go to what little was left of Sherwood Forest and even climb inside the ancient oak where Robin Hood and his "merry men" reputedly hid–out when the Sheriff of Nottingham happened to be passing. Fenced–off, protected and theme parked now.

Unlike the mock–Tudor estates that edged the road out of Mansfield to Nottingham, at least you could visit the aristocratic places at set times of the year and under certain restrictions, and thus contribute to the heating bills of the aristocracy, or help fill the coffers of the national "Trust". The merely prosperous estates en route, though intriguing, seemed more out of reach, these were private lanes, "No Buskers and Hawkers", "Private Property" and the plain "Keep Off" or "Keep Out" signs. So many warnings, I never really wanted to go in. Prosperous white–collar land.

Newstead Abbey was a favorite haunt; ruined cloisters, peacocks and a wishing well, a famous poet's family home; a short bus ride to a world that seemed so far from Garibaldi. An estate of course, is also what you make your mark with, what you leave and pass on. At the time I never discovered whether there was an extant Byron still at home, perhaps concealed in some closed–off corner?

What you pass on is not of course likely to be that much in the case of most estate "dwellers". An estate is a place you are expected to stay on in. If the state allows, you might get to own, or part–own, your allotted slice. But whether your estate's assets after liabilities form part of an inheritance, or whether your part of the estate is simply there for your lifetime and passed on to strangers after death, both forms of estate suggest a "settlement".

Permanence on offer, or worse, a form of responsibility; in part a responsibility towards "community".

When we moved onto the Coal Board estate, in the early 60s, there were six of us, and the dog, Laddie. My older sisters moved out after marriage, and I, local boy made good, moved on to College. During my time there, my parents died. By the early 70s, that left just my younger brother and the dog in a largish house on an almost exclusively family estate. Laddie got ill and had to be "put down". Kevin, who had perhaps had a few friends round to stay, was essentially left on his own. Kevin, who, like me, had not followed in his father's footsteps, not entered the metal cage – a place few outsiders ever see except when men emerge from a mining disaster on TV – had not gone down the pit. So many ghosts on "Gara", Kevin needed to leave, to take his place on a more neutral council list.

I was by then living in a student house, Cranham Terrace, an old terraced housing estate in an area mysteriously named "Jericho", though there were no walls, it felt enclosed and yet near to the centre of Oxford. A short walk to my college. Jericho, like Garibaldi, might have been built for particular local workers, the work had run out and gentrification had begun. Academics, students, arty types, were moving in. I haven't been back there for decades, I can imagine what those terraced houses"go for" now.

Hertford College had felt like another kind of estate; I had a room there in the first year, on an old staircase overlooking its Bridge of Sighs. There were sighs a–plenty in this then same sex college, some of them my own. The gate closed at midnight, but everyone knew there was always a basement window left open for us to climb back in through. The bar would almost certainly still be open, the chapel and the library were 24 hour. Another Oxford memoir, best resisted.

There was a year off though, a year "out". Part of it spent on a strangely isolated estate between Park Hospital, Headington, and across the field, the Warneford, a psychiatric hospital associated for me then with students who had cracked up, a friend or two included. Student attempts at suicide. But I was taken on as an assistant nurse, in the children's department, with its special concern for epilepsy, a condition that took so many and astonishing forms. I had read about Dostoevsky's epilepsy. As a child I used to drop down in the school "assembly" or in the street, and go as rigid as a board. Anyone passing might have concluded that I was dead. Working with epileptic children and finding out more about it led me to realise that I might have been epileptic myself. It was never diagnosed as such, I had something that I would "grow out of" my Mum had said the doctor said. I did though recently learn that my neurology remains unusual, and epilepsy can always return.

There was a sort of outhouse, or rather a row of outhouses, where the parents could stay over. A strange mix it was, adults in the old hospital on one side, a nurses' hostel in the middle, my more modern workplace was on the other. Some children had the obvious fits; other might just have a shake, a finger twitching for 24 hours a day. I saw a baby die; I helped give oxygen to another. I witnessed a lobotomy. The unit for parents to stay in was a complex place, it meant that they could be close to their children in the hospital, but it also meant that an array of doctors, nurses, psychiatrists and social workers could also keep an eye on them.

A hospital complex, a college campus, a prison complex, a religious order or an army barracks. Estates to take the mind off the solely domestic; with a greater potential for the erotic. It is not for nothing that so many films, television soaps and series, not to mention porn films, are so often set in or on them.

Colleges I still connect to, hospitals I might see more of, and I would be likely to resist any orders, military or religious. But there is always the fantasy of being a writer in residence.

Unsettled, restless, I once sent out an address change, "Paul has moved from Garden Road, to Bonington Road, to Kelvin Close, Mansfield to Hertford College, Cranham Terrace to St. Margaret's Road, Oxford, to Harley Street, St, Mary's Mansions, Hereford Road, Bethnal Green Road, Lynette Avenue, Thornhill Road, to Weston Rise Estate, and Hamlet's Way ..."

In London the area seemed more key, Bayswater, Bethnal Green, Soho, Peckham, West Ham, New Cross, Mile End, Islington, King's Cross,

Wimbledon, Tooting Broadway, with a few somewhat short stays in South-end and Bournemouth, even San Francisco.

The list was longer, and it went on and on.

Sometimes so close to homeless, yet seemingly unqualified for any waiting list at all, times when I would have taken almost any room anywhere. I would have given anything for the chance of my own estate flat. Almost any recognised and registered room would have done.

When not walking, it's a window I need. The first thing I look for in every place I consider a move to, not that I have always been able to be picky, is a room with a view. Nothing too scenic or remote, I want something near to the street. The countryside holds no interest for me, at least not after a second night. I prefer trees that push through in the city, even trees that appear half-choked by it.

I looked, over and over, at the photographs of Haggerston Estate taken for this book. I was gripped and touched, but realised I had little to say, no people to look at, though so many to imagine. But many of my "imagined" residents are alive, and some will move into the "regenerated" estate, once the existing one has been demolished.

Perhaps I might "lightly fictionalise"?
Base a story on the "evidence" of lives from the photographs, but also on the stories that were told to me?

It was a good send off. I didn't
expect that many to turn up. And most
of them made an effort at least. Ivy
was in a bit of a state. Gina was dolled up
to the eyebrows. Didn't think he would,
but Mark brought Ibrahim. I lost count
after the first twenty cars. Funny seeing
Jamilla's new car there, she said she'd
never set foot on the estate
again the day after they set fire to
her old one.
A present it was, for her finally getting
her Open University and it only
lasted two days. From her old Dad she
never thought she'd hear from again.
She never found out how he knew she'd
been studying. And he wasn't made of
money. She took one look at the car,
went straight round to Ivy's and asked
if she wouldn't mind opening up early.
She had her hair done, packed a bag,
and that was that.

And she stuck to her word, never came back for the furniture. Of course, that had gone by the next night anyway. Bastards took every last light socket, switch and bulb.

What would Ivy have made of it? Jim and Bill looked smart, amazing really, if you'd ever seen the state of their flat. I offered to give it a tidy once a week, but I could tell they were offended. What is it that Quentin Crisp said? "After the first four years, the dirt doesn't get any worse." So I let it rest.

But Kath had always kept it so spotless, pure Irish linen, always the best.

Jamilla gave me her old computer and taught me how to use it. Never thought I'd live to see the day. Just basic, but not bad at sixty! A mixed blessing if ever there was one. I felt like I was going abroad, and I never was one for going abroad much.

I definitely should not try to write like this, I concluded. I have always been thrown by local "memories", whether of the good old days or the bad ones, "voices" taped and transcribed. Some of the comment is of the "I can remember when it was safe to leave your door open" variety, a dubious tone of security. The idea that you are safe when you "know everyone" and your relatives surround you.

My taking a tone from them and mimicking their voices only made matters worse.

It is not just that many of the people there are still alive, some have moved, some have been re–housed; their stories are rich, but not always "tell–able". The ways people get by at times, the nature of their relationships, the restrictions due to libel laws, and even a fear. Some people might not take so kindly to their stories being messed with.

But more than that, I think the problem was that I said I would write an estate "story". The older I get, the less I feel like a fiction writer, though I spent so many years reading fiction, I was obsessed with fiction. Fiction seems to work for me when the writing is the starting–point, as in theatre or film, There, others take over. But fiction based on photographs already taken? I am still puzzling as to why I find this a problem, is it a problem with the "authentic" photograph? Probably not, since the photographs are so patterned.

The photographers kept, at my possibly foolish request, sending me news, feeding me stories. I found the tales riveting and troubling in equal measure.

After my Dad died when I was 11, I went on what was called at the time the "Country Holiday Fund", I think it was run through the council and school, for 'the poor kids'.

Me and another girl from the flats stayed on a farm at a place called Market Harborough. We had a good time. There were cows and pigs and he kept bees so we used to watch him take the honeycomb from the hives and put it in a sort of spinner, sorry can't remember much more.

T, the guy they found dead in the flat, had lived without electricity for five years, he refused to pay the bill.

Living here so long, I saw the first live–work lofts and the general gentrification of the area. I remember the burnt out cars that were dumped here so frequently and how they suddenly were used as a way to resist gentrification, New Labour toffs moving into what was called a working class area. Why, when this place is about to go, do I feel the urge to hold onto something, to see for the first time in 13 years that there is a hairdressers on the estate called "Helen's".

No one wanted her life–long collection of mismatching but most delicate drinking glasses, so sad. The precarious life? The meaninglessness of it all?

Not sure if we told you about the work–house, full of porn, we came across a guy in one of the flats. Basically the workers had pried open the orange boards and moved in, wired the place up. They had no natural light, but all else. Mattress next to mattress, and lots of porn. The guy was injured and shaking all over. He had a bandage around him. So the ambulance came and said "Thank God you found him," and took him to hospital.

She said she finds it hard to think of Haggerston as a desirable place to live. She felt there was something very prison–like in the design of those types of estate. Very exposed but little in creating an architectural sense of community. Not as bad as the tower blocks, but cold and institutional. She kept longing for some curves and green amongst the brown brick lines. I always loved the open access and the red bricks and even the way it spreads out. I think she perhaps needs to live in a house.

Forget fiction, especially the "local". The piece, I thought, should be an essay. What was I doing trying to create funny, heated and moving scenes? The attempts to base a story "loosely based on" the tales of the estate, the tales I have been told, just descended into sentimental drivel. I tried reducing the text to a few fragments.

Loosely based on the stories I have been told ...

Or fiction based purely on the photographs themselves, lives lived, the painted cross, the old cassettes or records not worth giving away, pop stars loved and football teams supported, the occasional ornament, even a painting or two, the free calendar from a takeaway, dried flowers, a comedy of patterns or degrees of dirt around the switches, the array of abandoned fireplaces, surprisingly few clothes, handles in states of disrepair, unsightly pipes, attempts to hide those pipes, unwanted lamps, old keys, walking aids, lists and reminders and a few words pinned to doors, shelves or magnet–attached to an abandoned fridge.

Little that looks accidentally left behind, forgotten.

A sense of the checks and double–checks, the decisions made on what was simply not worth taking.

Some things dealt with, some just patched over, but mostly the sense of the unresolved, a problem there was perhaps no interest, time, energy, ability or assistance to fix, a giving up, perhaps. Or was it rather that people were being given up on?

Cool and bordering the ethnographic, impersonal, made bearable, and even funny, by the repetition of the camera position in flat after flat. The photographs seemed best left alone. Why try to finish something when the very sense was of nothing ever quite finished?

A few clues, the odd poster or magazine, though the flats were to be boarded, concreted up and demolished, almost nothing of the erotic.

From embarrassment that a builder you will never see might see it?
Or do you continue to hold onto it all, or destroy it on making a fresh start?
Was it always hidden anyway from the family, the flatmate, the lover?

No sense of the sex lives of the tenants, though you could certainly imagine the occasional crime scene investigation.

This feels different to my usual walks and windows, watching and wanting to be invisible; the almost total absence of the erotic, it disturbs me. Every memory of every place I have lived in is, after all, mostly erotic.

New estates, "regeneration" and the nearness to the idea of the "gated community", but with an "appropriate" mix; or "pepper potting" as I am told this is known. A mix might make the property values drop, even if socially the new owners might quite like it. A mix of temporary residents, "affordable" housing for "key workers" and space for regular home–owning ones.

That attempt was tried before, nurses were added in. They soon, feeling intimidated, moved on.

The same stories of violence, drugs and drink amongst
the newer home–owning residents, but their stories are less naked, more carefully concealed.

From nosey caretakers observing your every move and your every guest, through to CCTV. Footage mostly useful after the fact. Coded cards, security guards. Every step monitored.

I have never felt truly secure on an estate and no amount of monitoring, seclusion or exclusion works for me.

The moments when you are so messed up, no one and no machine seems able to help.

"He is in a right state" or "It's his nerves" as the gossips speaking over the garden walls on Ladybrook, Mansfield might have said.

The past – cherish, discard, retrieve, involuntarily search for it, reinvent, work it out of the system, ditch it and block sender, leave friends and loves disunited or even deleted? I don't know what to do with my own, let alone the pasts of others.

Police were called to an estate today ... A senior minister today visited an estate in ... Pop star R later visited the estate she was brought up on ... A triumphant tennis star today returned ... The tragic story for one family on the estate ... Residents complained ... A terror suspect was ... The last ...

Papers concerning the occupation of the Haggerston estates by Lieutenant Thomas Love of Tynemouth Castle and their subsequent sequestration and sale by the Commissioners to Messrs John Brownell and Gilbert Crouch for £3,000, who demised them back to Thomas Haggerston in 1653.

I moved to Haggerston after I had split up with my partner ... it was quite a transitional time for me. I had shared the two-bedroom flat temporarily with three other people: a couple and a friend. So, it was cozy! Was calm in the early days – 1990 or 1991 – and then got crazy in about 1995 – 1997. I'd have to recheck my dates, but that's what I recall. It was a long struggle to get on the tenancy list. By that time I just wanted to leave ...

Yes, that's the name of the video they made here in response to the drug problems, Haggerston, It's Not Just Heroin. Apparently this was the 'heroin capital' of England ... surely overstated but anyway, they made this when I moved into Pamela House.

... when I explained this project to her she declared, looking slightly horrified, "Oh I've been in a council flat once! They are not too bad."

Her husband, now long dead, loved his car. In the early days of the CCTV technology he was a pioneer, mounting cameras in his kitchen window and above the front door to keep a protective eye at the car parked outside his flat. Anything coming close to the car such as footballs etc. was confiscated promptly, never to be returned to its rightful owner.

Who is stealing the pipes and the water tanks? N says that the gypsies come in vans and break into the bricked–up flats to steal the water tanks to sell them off to the scrap yard down the road. U and R said that people come pretending that they are from the Water Board and take out the tanks to sell them on to the scrap yard for 100 squid. K says that it is the council that takes out the water tanks of the bricked–up flats to put them in other flats to exchange faulty ones.

There is a knitting club, free internet facilities for elderly people, regular social events, music workshops.

Strange Fruit: The food coop is run entirely by volunteers. One of the West Indian women made them aware that the name actually means dead bodies dangling from a tree, people murdered by the KKK.

A famous bank robbery was apparently planned on the estate … I found reference to its planning and rendition into an Oscar winning 1948 film, Odd Man Out, or some such, where an unnamed Irish resistance organisation wanted to replenish its funds.

Infestations. Haggerston, the biotope.

Police raids. The police raided S's flat instead of the one next to her. "Paul, just now there are 20 police outside, some with purple rubber gloves, when did they start wearing the purple ones?"

The picture of a happy snoozing dog having destroyed a couch (see opposite) is from J. That was his dog when he could still walk well … He could tell you each kind of brick, and in particular the older ones where the cement was a bit brittle, he would be able to make a hole and climb through.

She and her husband moved into the 'prestige blocks' in 1953. She has to move soon. When she moved in, it was during the Queen's coronation, and her and her husband bought 53 carnations, and they placed the plant pots outside their flat, in a little green patch. One by one, the plants disappeared. One day her husband came back by another route and found that their neighbour had many pots of carnations in her living room window. They never confronted the neighbour …

She won repeated awards on local gardening competitions and the Hackney Gazette ran an article in 1975 called "A bright spot in a dark place". When the new landlords took over they cut down her garden. She came home one day from visiting her son, and all that was left were brown stumps. This was in winter 2008/9 The builders said finally, "You can see the road again, now it's safe for you." The new landlords claimed that health and safety regulations mean that this was standard; there could be no shrubbery on the estate apart from in designated areas. The Hackney Gazette ran an article called "Call this Pruning?" The new landlord apologised and employed a gardener to restore her garden. They put in many plants and now she only complains about the condoms and nappies thrown into it from the flat above.

Perhaps estates are always in decline, the ideals and ideas behind them being so grand.

The uncertainty of the street seems preferable, and everyone is to be seen there, even if some of them only step from a taxi to a department store. Every chance encounter on every street where no one knows much about you. You are just what they see, if they notice you at all, and only what they can guess at.

I feel at once faithful to and a traitor to the estates I was placed in, or those I merely paused on.

A kind of guilt, or sense of failure, in the wandering, though I am never quite sure what the "charge" might be, or why I did not pass the test and settle.

I fear the last estate, the retirement home. The old upholstered armchairs, though so many look decoratively out to sea. Most housing estates I found myself wanting to leave almost immediately on arrival. Too many domestic stories, stories of the damaged, I see and am touched, but I do not really want to look too closely.

I can't really share in the fascination of the issues that surround estates.

Housing, so far from the world of work, so separate.

The only pleasure was in watching the comings and goings from a window. Or the chance view from a window. People at home, people passing; their rituals and routines.

Every estate I feel as a place I will be caught on or caught out in.

I should start on a store of walking sticks and canes.

I need to leave the estate, and thank you, I can find my own way out.

And yet, there is a spirit.

Apparently, when the Turkish "guest–workers" arrived to work in Germany in the 1960–70s, though mostly poor, they still had to phone home.

One of them, perhaps examining the sparse facilities of the estate, came up with a solution.

Make money from ice to fit the coin boxes.

The calls lasted till the ice melted.

For a long time the German telecom people were perplexed. How was it that the coin boxes could be empty and yet show no sign of being broken into? There was no sign of any counterfeit coin.

And if that is but an urban legend, what matter.

Archaeology of the Recent Past

A Reflection on Knowledge Production

Victor Buchli

The archaeology of the 'recent past' occupies a certain ambiguous position, as the term suggests, which is inherently part of its productive power. Focusing on what are oftentimes the forgotten, underfoot, unnoticed, unremarked upon or overlooked, the objects of archaeologies of the recent past are rarely claimed by historians or preservationists. In this sense it is precisely that which is unclaimed, the abject and wasted that makes it available for appropriation. Yet the archaeology of the recent past is also by definition almost always concerned with the painful and forgotten aspects of recent experience and other elements of social life that fall out of dominant discourses. This is so for the simple reason that the sites of these experiences are oftentimes those that are too difficult to engage with or represent in the present through conventional media or are simply beyond their scope. These are experiences such as recent wartime atrocities, civil conflict, homelessness and other forms of social dispossession or circumstance that are too painful, too volatile or too ephemeral to express otherwise. Such an archaeology is thus well suited to voice and materialise the experiences of those individuals who might normally be excluded by dominant discourses through the archaeological act's ability to constitute materially and discursively that which could not be constituted before. It is precisely the abject nature of the objects of an archaeology of the recent past that makes them radically available. This is part of such an archaeology's productive power and why it can be unsettling, destabilising and even threatening at times through its capacity to render the familiar strange and critically constitute the previously un-constitutable, thereby forging an engagement where previously there was none. It is this ambiguous and unclaimed position that draws archaeologists wishing to consider new modes of practice in relation to the unspoken and un-constituted experiences of the recent past. And it is precisely these experiences that also attract art practitioners such as those at work here at the Haggerston Estate. While both sets of practices (the archaeological and the artistic) overlap in terms of object, and at times also in terms of their material and temporal frames, neither practices in their conventional forms can lay a claim on this territory – it is available, open and volatile. In these respects, the recent past offers working material for both sets of practices within the productive mode of so–called 'composting actions' that permit the renewal of cultural life, as described by the anthropologist Mary Douglas.[1]

Archaeology as intervention and creative practice

This overlap between creative art practice and archaeological practice is by no means new. Traditionally artistic practice and archaeological practice were not as distinct as they are now conventionally conceived. Raphael was renowned as an artist, architect and archaeologist, and was responsible for the first archaeological surveys of Rome. His archaeology of Roman ruins was instrumental in the development of his architecture, for example in the Villa Madama, as shown by Alessandro Zambelli.[2] Similarly 18th–century architects working within the emerging scholarly traditions of Roman and Greek antiquity were avid archaeologists and recorders of these works, constituting the antique and creating reconstructions as part of their own design practice in the pursuit of neo–classicism in the contemporary architectural practice of the time. Traditionally we think of a sharp contrast between the discipline of archaeology and the discipline of art/architecture as emerging with their increasing professionalisation and autonomy in the 19th century. However, echoes of this earlier preoccupation with archaeology by architects can be found in the most avowedly modernist work of the 20th century. For such masters as Le Corbusier, an appreciation of the ruins of prehistoric forms was crucial for the invention of modernist principles.[3] Architects and designers have studied the remains of so–called primordial forms in order to re–establish and renew the conventions of architectural practices, from the neo–classicists, modernists and constructivists to the preoccupation with vernacular and prehistoric forms in the present.[4] Undercurrents linking the two disciplines, though normally held apart, can be characterised as having varying degrees of overt association historically. More recently artists[5] and archaeologists[6] have found themselves in a similar dialogue which concerns a consistent reworking of techniques, interventions and representations common to anthropology and architecture, such as the site report, catalogue, exhibition, participant observation, survey etc. Flora Vilches has argued that both artists and archaeologists, under the influence of post–modern philosophical thought, have found themselves occupying similar intellectual territory with a similar pre–disposition towards the critical analysis of problems where both archaeological work and art practice are seen as contemporary interventions that are politically motivated, and whose work must be directly attuned as a critical social practice with the means it has at its disposal.[7]

There is some precedence for this during the early pre–Stalinist Soviet period, when a similar philosophical ground and political activism witnessed and even required a convergence in thinking and mutual engagement. This was a period when 'art for art's sake' was abandoned by Marxist thinkers in favour of a socially engaged practice that would permeate all aspects of social life, in effect a practice that was avowedly and socially efficacious. This ambivalence towards the dominance of aesthetics in the western tradition is echoed in the later anthropological work of Alfred Gell, which argues for the consideration of artistic practice outside of the conventional western aesthetic debates and more in terms of its ability to effect social relations.[8] In the case of the Soviet Union, this was to directly facilitate revolution and social change. Back then Soviet artists, architects, designers, ethnologists and sociologists were linked through a common goal of social reform and a common body of social theory that attempted to understand, historically and in the present, the social and material conditions of life that might be refigured in the future. In the realm of archaeology and architecture, practitioners were concerned with critical interventions that attempted to discern and constitute the material forms of social reform. Both disciplines in effect saw themselves as critically analysing and constituting the material terms of social life, retrodictively in the case of archaeology and predictively in the case of architecture.[9]

More recently the emphasis on performance, public engagement and temporary intervention reveals common points of contact between archaeologists and art practitioners. In particular Vilches singles out the work of Robert Smithson, Fred Miller, Susan Hillier and Mark Dion. The engagement between archaeology and artistic practice is most overt in Dion's work. He specifically conducts what appear to be mock archaeological digs, surveys, labs, reports and exhibitions that subtly mock the archaeological method and typologies to offer a critique of archaeological practice itself, while at the same time attesting to the transfigurative and critical power of archaeology to create and transform existing categories of thought in new and distinctive ways.

The compliment is returned by archaeologists, such as Chris Tilley and others, who attempt ephemeral interventions in the remnants of the pre–historic landscape, such as bright coloured wrapping over stones, to suggest new categories of interpretation and typology in reference to alternative phenomenologically inspired understandings of the landscape. These interventions, inspired by art practices, challenge existing archaeological categories and are suggestive of radically new interpretive frames. Within these practices one can discern many resonances with the works of Richard Long, Andrew Goldsworthy and others, as the archaeologist Colin Renfrew has observed. Both sets of practices have many points in common in terms of the formal and interpretive frame of understanding prehistoric and contemporary landscapes.[10]

These practices exploit similar media, and even method. The work of both archaeologists and anthropologists is primarily textual or curatorial – media that are relatively constrained compared to the primarily visual and more embodied phenomenological media (i.e. performance etc.) in which art practitioners work. However, archaeologists, anthropologists and artists share certain common ground in all these media: the textual and visual practices of archaeological and anthropological site reports, monographs and documentary evidence have points in common with art practitioners (such as Landy, Dion, Hillier, Boltanski and others) who consciously reprise these conventions. Similarly, while the field site as theatrical performance has a limited role in archaeological practice[11] and is almost negligible in ethnographic practice – except in so much as we might understand the notion of the ethnographic encounter between ethnographer and informant as analogous to the performance artist with his or her audience – in these different contexts the encounter actually produces the work either through the performance event or the ethnographic encounter later creatively documented and circulated as a monograph. These are distinctly collaborative events, albeit inherently asymmetrical, sustained through the unfolding of time within a specific space. The spaces and temporal frames in turn produce specific forms of knowledge that are at the heart of all these forms of practice, as well as a particular emphasis on the author/creator as singular authority in terms of their asymmetry despite the wider social and collaborative character of their work.

What is interesting is the nature of the common ground that these practices often occupy. Such ground is typically the unclaimed, abject and therefore more widely available for intervention, falling outside of established disciplinary concerns, practices and even legal categories where questions of cultural heritage are concerned. For the archaeologist such sites do not constitute what we think of conventionally as heritage and are therefore not subject to preservation laws and practices. Archaeologists are therefore able to work in far more experimental ways, as Schofield, Harrison, Moshenska, De Silvey and others have done in contexts that are thought of as 'run–down' or 'blighted' or of little interest to the conventional concerns of heritage practice because they are too recent, too modern or seemingly uninteresting.[12] It is precisely the abject nature of these sites – such as Haggerston Estate – forgotten by the powers that be, that leave them available for reuse and renewal in radically new and challenging ways. Such sites are simultaneously the symptom and the cure of the neglected, painful or blighted aspects of recent experience. At its best, this work is not a formal typological exercise or critique – the pursuit of some formal and romanticised aesthetic problem for its own sake – but a conscious effort to constitute new objects and frames of reference in terms of interventions that draw attention and focus outwards towards an alternative vision of life and community, and which forms the basis upon which a renewed sense of community and place can emerge.

Composting effects

Mary Douglas speaks of the composting effects of what various societies describe, in their distinctive terms, as waste. Anthropologists and archaeologists such as Laurence Douny, Caitlin De Silvey, Gavin Lucas and others speak about the seemingly abject as a special resource that must be husbanded precisely for its ability to facilitate renewal.[13] What in conventional western terms might be thought of as waste is actually a resource to be cared for and nurtured. Part of the ability of such waste to be considered as a resource has to do with the inherent quality of waste and other abject things as being caught between indigenous categories: neither immediately socially useful nor completely disintegrated and useless. Its liminal status is what makes it available for other radical purposes, and within that lies its generative potential and productive power, which suggest new uses and associations with the productive implications that such entropic processes engender. De Silvey elegantly describes the creative and generative instability of substance through the entropic processes at play in decaying Montana homesteads and their productive capacities to suggest new relations between people and things, landscape and architecture, nature and culture.[14] Rejecting the conventions of preservation and conservation practices that would halt, reverse or sanitise these processes, she instead argues persuasively to let these entropic processes simply be – decaying in place with the lessons they elicit – precisely for their creative effects and radical reworking of established typologies. Being contingently rendered outside and abject, according to the specific requirements of a given cultural setting, such 'abject' things are thus available to suggest other generative uses.

The dialogue that occurs between archaeological and artistic practices when engaging these similar objects and sites becomes a remarkably fruitful one. This is not due to any overt collaboration – such direct interaction would probably stymie such effects. As both practices are direct social interventions, their mutual engagement can only augment and critique each other's activity. However, the products and artefacts of such activities can work well beyond mutual critique and can function as important objects beyond the confines of their respective practices. For instance, the juridical status of such objects is not to be underestimated especially when considering wider cultural and social claims. It is certainly the case that the visual and material culture of groups cast as artistic outputs are the basis upon which claims for integrity and rights are maintained, particularly amongst indigenous groups in the United States, Canada, Australia and elsewhere. It is also certainly the case that anthropological texts function to serve such claims in court cases regarding restitution and land claims.

What both practices do, as has been noted in studies within the archaeology of the recent past, is to objectify discursively, performatively and vis-ually – in short, to make 'visible' that which is oftentimes not constituted and forgotten. This emphasis on the visual and material register is significant. The disciplines of archaeology and anthropology at their 19th century points of origins were a melancholic attempt to save the remnants of vanished cultures and vanishing cultures, especially those coming under the control of expanding globalising colonial economies and disappearing in their wake. Small objects, drawings etc., were the media whose material affordances in terms of portability and scale enabled collection, categorisation, comparison and transportation from colonial peripheries to imperial capitals, where they became the so–called 'object lessons' that enabled the emerging sciences of anthropology and archaeology. 'Things' became 'material culture', functioning in a fashion entirely alien to their original intents, to enable this melancholic work and render these distant, disappearing and disappeared cultures knowable and observable to the colonial metropolitan centre. These objectifications take on an important social life either as legal instruments to rectify wrongs, or as flash points about which new convergences and forms of community can arise. These objects, which are in effect that which is 'thrown out' as the etymology of the word suggests,[15] become the means by which the various assemblies that form around these 'objects'[16] in the social, material and juridical sense become possible – 'thrown out' as such, they are generative. Such 'objects' of course, depending on their particular material affordances, are dynamic or one might say unstable. Amenable to appropriation in terms of their particular affordances and determining in an unfixed but non–arbitrary way the forms of assembly, knowledge and community they permit, they are in these respects 'promiscuous', as Nicholas Thomas once suggested.[17] In short they are available to be used in unexpected ways and with unexpected implications for the non–arbitrary 'assemblies' they might then enable, such as unexpected but distinctive forms of social life.

However, these 'objects' as produced within an archaeology of the recent past are also inherently 'unreasonable'. The melancholic artefacts of the 19th century refuse to submit to the inexorable processes of colonial expansion and modernisation, just as the artefacts produced by archaeologies of the recent past refuse to submit to the inexorable processes of rapid change and the superfluity of information that characterise contemporary life and obscure the mute and unconstituted experiences of the dispossessed, abject, underfoot and silenced. Rather, in turn, practices 'erupt' to challenge such settlements. As Eng and Kazanjian have suggested elsewhere, melancholy as an 'unreasonable' refusal constitutes a direct attempt to engage the world in other ways against the inexorable processes of 'progress', 'modernisation' or 'reform' or the settlements enforced by established narratives and histories.[18]

This is why when archaeologies of the contemporary past have been conducted they have been rather successful in forging new forms of sociality and community through the course of the archaeological intervention. Moshenska's work amongst school children in relation to World War II shelters created an awareness of place and local history that became the focus of new forms of community identification in terms of the history and local narratives of the community and their families regarding the experience of the war.[19] This archaeological intervention served to supplant 'official' histories with more relevant local and intimate ones – making national histories local, and using local histories to challenge national ones. Similarly, Layla Renshaw's work as a forensic archaeologist in rural Spain, investigating the exhumation of the civil war dead, shows how such interventions address long simmering tensions and produce new terms by which local history, community and its future might develop.[20] Here the particular visual and material affordances of excavated artefacts and the visual representations served to specifically facilitate certain kinds of identifications that structured the agonistic process of reconciliation, and the rewriting of local history and national narrative. Rodney Harrison's work amongst Australian Aboriginal communities facilitated a reconnection and elaboration of indigenous narratives of place and familial lineage in a setting that fell between the cracks of recent memory and the limits of traditional heritage practice.[21] Through innovative and unobtrusive tracking and documentation techniques, Harrison's interventions provided and created new objects and landscapes of objects through which these claims could be articulated and sustained. An otherwise forgotten sense of recent Aboriginal history and dislocation could be reclaimed and sustained to produce alternative narratives to the ones prevailing within the 'modernising' discourse of recent Australian history and 'reform' practices. *In Wait*, with its insistence on looking at the last 'troubled' 30 years at Haggerston, is such an attempt by artist practitioners to conduct what may be considered an archaeology of the recent past.

The 'objects' produced in the highly dynamic field of the abject, in which such artists, archaeologists and anthropologists work, lend themselves to appropriation. The artists/archaeologists/anthropologists produce mediated encounters in time with their respective communities. The exhibition, the installation, the preserved site, the site report, the photo essay, or other such work, all take on distinct roles, in keeping with their material affordances, in terms of the future relations or assemblies they illicit or can be marshalled to create, often in unexpected ways. These are avowedly creative interventions whose success can be discerned in their wider effects. Not any intervention will do. Some are simply banal; some are formalistic or aestheticised, while others can be quite strategic and effective in terms of the objects constituted, the issues raised and the communities engaged and forged. In this respect, there is a deliberate element of political intervention that is informed by the political issues at hand and the media used, be it either archaeological or artistic. Overt collaboration may not be fruitful but a sympathetic engagement, which has a synergistic effect and reach, emerges naturally as the different practitioners approach the same issues and sites. These cross–disciplinary engagements offer valuable insights and critiques into each other's forms of practice, generating further objects with unexpected uses, both between them and amongst the communities and audiences they engage with. The Haggerston Project ably shows these effects with a critical felicity.

1. V. Buchli and G. Lucas, *Archaeologies of the Contemporary Past* (London: Routledge,2001).
2. A. Zambelli, 'Villa Madama and the Scandalous Practice of Raffaello Sanzio', paper delivered at Christ Church College, University of Oxford, 13 June 2009.

3. A. Vogt, *Le Corbusier, the noble savage: toward an archaeology of modernism* (Cambridge MA: MIT press, 1998); J. Rykwert, 'Positive and Arbitrary', in *On Adam's House in Paradise: The Idea of the Primitive Hut in Architectural History* (Cambridge, MA: MIT Press, 1986).
4. V. Buchli, 'Constructing Utopian Sexualities: the Archaeology and Architecture of the Early Soviet State', in R. Schmidt and B. Voss (eds), *Archaeologies of Sexuality* (London: Routledge, 2000); A. Rappoport, *House Form and Culture* (Englewood Hills, NJ: Prentice Hall, 1969); P. Oliver, *Dwellings: The House across the world* (Oxford: Phaidon, 1987).
5. For example the work of Michael Landy, Richard Long, Robert Smithson, Christian Boltanski, Mark Dion, Sophie Calle, Cornelia Parker and Susan Hillier.
6. Various archaeologists have been inspired directly and indirectly by analogous methods taken from artistic practice such Michael Shanks, Christopher Tilley, Colin Renfrew,Michael Parker–Pearson, de Silvey and my colleague Gavin Lucas and myself.
7. F. Vilches, 'The Art of Archaeology: the Archaeological Process in the Work of Robert Smithson, Mark Dian and Fred Wilson', PhD dissertation, Faculty of the Graduate School of the University of Maryland, College Park, 2002.
8. A. Gell, 'The Maori Meeting House', in *Art and Agency: An Anthropological Theory* (Oxford: Oxford University Press, 1988) pp. 251–258.
9. *ibid.*, Buchli (2000).
10. B. Bender, S. Hamilton & C. Tilley, *Stone Worlds: Narrative and Reflexivity in Landscape Archaeology* (Walnut Creek, CA: Left Coast Press, 2007); C. Renfrew, *Figuring it Out* (London: Thames and Hudson, 2003).
11. M. Pearson and M. Shanks, *Theatre/Archaeology* (London: Routledge, 2001); M. Shanks, 'Three Rooms: Archaeology and Performance', *Journal of Social Archaeology*, 4(2), 2004, pp. 147–180.
12. John Schofield, 'Intimate Engagements: Art, Heritage and Experience at the "Place–Ballet"', *International Journal of the Arts in Society*, 1(5), 2007, pp. 105–114; R. Harrison, 'The archaeology of "lost places": ruin memory and the heritage of the aboriginal diaspora in Australia', *Historic Environment*, 17(1), 2003, pp. 18–22; G. Mochenska, 'Second World War Archaeology in Schools: A Backdoor to the History Curriculum?', *Papers from the Institute of Archaeology*, 19, 2009; Caitlin De Silvey, 'Observed Decay: Telling Stories with Mutable Things', *Journal of Material Culture*, 11, 2006, pp. 318–333.
13. L. Douny, 'The Materiality of Domestic Waste: The Recycled Cosmology of the Dogon, of Mali', *Journal of Material Culture*, 12(3), 2007, pp. 309–331; *ibid.*, De Silvey (2006); Gavin Lucas, 'Disposability and Dispossession in the Twentieth Century', *Journal of Material Culture*, 7(1), 2002, pp. 5–22.
14. *ibid.*, De Silvey (2006).
15. I am grateful to Pwyl ab Stiffin for this observation from Lorrain Daston's work.
16. As suggested in the work of Bruno Latour.
17. N. Thomas, *Entangled Objects: Exchange, Material Culture and Colonialism in the Pacific* (Cambridge Mass.: Harvard University Press, 1991).
18. D. L. Eng and D. Kazanjian (eds), Loss (Berkeley: University of California Press, 2003).
19. *ibid.*, Moshenska (2009).
20. Layla Renshaw, 'Bodies near at hand: the dissonant memory and dormant graves of the Spanish Civil War', in Bille et al., *The Anthropology of Absence: Materializations of Transcendance and Loss* (New York: Springer, 2010).
21. *ibid.*, Harrison (2003).

What Now?

Reflections on what public housing has been and could become

Cristina Cerulli

"Prospective tenants were easily wooed by the promise of higher technical standards, particularly of plumbing and sanitation, which enticed them even into high-rise flats, where disillusionment subsequently and often quickly set in ... The whole operation was a culture transfer amounting to a cultural colonization: a vision forged by one section of society for application to another, to whom it might be more, or less, acceptable and appropriate. The tenure and design, together were instruments of social reform; but this did not carry any special programme over and above that implicit in the original inspiration. It asked nothing more of tenants than to live in the houses and to participate in estate life in ways approved by middle class reformers."[1]

This essay is a reflection on issues surrounding the current, past and future life of existing public housing, and an exploration of what new public housing provision could be. The premise is that public housing is highly political and that any attempt to understand its history and its spatial manifestations should acknowledge this political nature.

Origins

The origins of British council housing have been traced, by many commentators, in both the response to conditions created by the industrial revolution and a wide range of utopian experiences such as communitarian experiments and cooperatives. The poor living conditions of the working classes in the late 19th century were the trigger for a number of projects and initiatives, such as the construction of workers' model industrial villages by 'benevolent' members of the upper classes. These villages in particular, and the garden city movement that grew out of them, were to become the spatial blueprint for 20th-century council housing, while the ideological under-pinning could be traced in upper-class feelings and beliefs about poverty.[2]

Before the end of World War I the government's attitude towards housing provision was rather laissez faire and the major parties were reluctant 'to increas[e] the role of the state in tackling poor housing and poverty',[3] supporting state intervention only when poor housing posed a major threat to public health.

The Addison Act, in 1919, allowed the building of new houses after World War I and marked the beginning of the 20th-century tradition of state-owned housing, which would much later evolve into council estates. The Act followed the Tudor Walters Committee Report, commissioned by Parliament in 1917, to explore the provision of housing and to create the foundations of post-war reconstruction. Partly prompted by the poor fitness conditions of many army recruits from urban areas during World War I[4] and by fears of working class agitation,[5] the work of the committee was steered by Raymond Unwin – the influential architect and urbanist behind Rowntree's model village at New Earswick and the garden city at Letchworth – and was heavily influenced Garden City ideals. The Addison Act was greeted with euphoria by the working classes but once threats of an uprising had ceased to be pressing the provision of quality housing for those in need became less of a priority, and in 1921, after animated Cabinet battles, 'repaying war debts' prevailed over 'social welfare' and the housing programme was cut (Addison resigned from the Cabinet).[6]

During the 1930s the emphasis shifted from the supply of what was called 'general needs' housing to slum clearance and redevelopment. The standards and quality of state-provided housing were progressively reduced and the supply of housing for owner occupation by private developers increased, fuelled by rising prosperity and availability of finances from building societies. After World War II, housing was part of the integrated effort of reconstruction, which was concerned with the physical environment and well as social fabric and economy. "In line with the principles of the emerging welfare state, it was felt that it was the public sector that should be the main provider of new housing",[7] and following the recommendations of the Dudley Report (1944) that called for an improvement of minimum standards, after the war the state embarked on the largest council housing building programme ever carried out in the UK and which is considered by many as the highest quality ever achieved in public housing.[8] An emergency phase of temporary housing using prefabricated units[9], immediately after the war, was followed by a steady programme of local authority building: between 1946 and 1957 a total of 2.5 million new houses and flats were built, 75% of which were council owned.

With the Conservatives back in power once again, the 1950s saw cuts that led to a reduction in both quality and quantity of housing supply. Concerns were growing about the appropriateness of low-density housing, paving the way for the rise of system-built high-rise blocks, towards which local authorities were attracted by the incentives of additional subsidies.[10] Housing-quality concerns were also growing and the Parker Morris Committee was set up to provide recommendations that would become mandatory for council housing from 1969 to 1981.[11] By the 1970s, the shortcomings of the 'clean sweep' approach to planning[12] became apparent and dissatisfaction with high-rise estates was on the up. General dissatisfaction about the demolition of old buildings and communities alike also generated a series of initiatives including "measures by the government to conserve historic environments and buildings, to ensure greater public participation in planning, and to replace the policy of slum clearance and new build with programmes of rehabilitations and improvement".[13] At the same time housing associations assumed a more prominent role. While 19th-century housing associations had pioneered housing provision for working-class tenants, they had played a relatively marginal role in the interwar period. From the early 1960s, a number of new housing associations were set up. The most renowned of these was the Notting Hill Housing Trust, headed by a charismatic minister whose first fundraising appeal, hinging around photos of a family with six children sharing a single-room dwelling, generated an overwhelming response[14].

In the council housing expansion years, from 1919 to 1971, housing provision was delegated by the central government to local authorities and it was subsidised to make rents affordable to most working–class tenants. The alternation of Labour and Conservative governments throughout the last hundred years has seen a sequence of progressive attempts at state housing provision usually followed by more reactionary policies that placed the emphasis on private provision. For most of the 20th century the two dominant types of housing were owner occupation, which was the tenure of choice and supported by easy access to finance and tax incentives, and council housing, for the working class, who had no option of owning a home.

The 1974 Housing Act enabled registered housing associations to provide subsidised homes and started a period when housing associations played an important role in housing provision, especially in the renovation of existing stock. The role of housing associations was viewed by the Labour Party as complementary to that of local authorities, and by the Conservatives as a substitute for the local authorities. Another Conservative government from 1979 meant yet another sharp change of direction towards home ownership, epitomised by Thatcher's right–to–buy legislation (1980 Housing Act). It can be argued that the increasing popularity of housing associations, boosted by 1974 Housing Act, in conjunction with the right–to–buy policy of 1980 Housing Act, contributed significantly to the decline of council housing.

The 1988 Housing Act was to be another crucial moment in housing associations' history. Although aimed at reducing their dependence on publicly funded capital subsidies and the consequent need to resort to private finance to support development programmes, the 1988 Housing Act also paved the way for a new major institutional role that housing associations were to play in housing provision. For the previous 25 years there had been general consensus in both Conservative and Labour Parties that local authorities were not performing well as landlords and that they should therefore give up this role. The sustained increase in the capital expenditure of housing associations and their growing track record in developing and managing housing made them "a credible alternative to council housing" and seemingly "more efficient and responsive landlords than local housing departments".[15] The government was now keen for housing associations to take on council housing stock and started to make arrangements for a Housing Stock Transfer Programme of estates where the majority of tenants supported the transfer in a formal ballot. A fierce Defend Council Housing Campaign was initiated and lobbied to stop housing stock transfer, which was seen as a form of privatisation, by encouraging tenants to vote 'no' in the ballots. Widespread opposition, beyond the Defend Council Housing Campaign, towards the transfer of ownership led to the introduction of a new option in 2002, the Arm's Length Management Organisation (ALMO), through which local authorities could transfer stock management without giving up ownership. A study was made in 2003 of the impact, real and perceived, of housing stock transfer, comparing performance data as well as analysing interviews with those involved in and affected by stock transfer. The study highlights stakeholders' perception that 'housing management performance (and average tenant satisfaction)' usually improve following stock transfer, but it also, however, flags up that there is "no clear evidence for the belief that transfer housing associations, as a class of landlords, outperform comparable local authorities".[16] In the same year, inspections carried out by the Housing Inspectorate showed that "the best housing authorities compare well with the best registered social landlords (RSLs)".[17]

Decline

> *" ... you only have to say the word 'estates' for someone to infer a vast amount of meaning from it. It's a bruise in the form of a word: it hits the nerves that register shame, disgust, fear and, very occasionally fierce pride."*[18]

A study on the stigma associated with living in council estates, entitled *Challenging Images,* highlights important cultural issues related to council estates.[19] As part of this study a researcher posed as a key worker trying to buy a flat in the proximity of a hospital so that she could walk to work. The obvious choice in terms of affordability and proximity would have been a particular estate, with an infamous reputation, just a short walk from the hospital; any other affordable location beyond that would involve a longer commute. Despite the 'problem' estate being the obvious choice, the estate agent did not mention it as an option and, when asked about it, he was adamant that she should avoid the estate, even just for an exploratory visit: "I wouldn't recommend any young female to be there."[20]

In 1934 in Cutteslowe, Oxford, Urban Housing Estate developed private housing on land purchased from the council and built the infamous wall around the council estate to protect the value of its development. The wall only came down in 1959, after growing protests and various unofficial attempts to demolish it, and it became the embodiment of the discrimination against council tenants: "a physical symbol of class prejudice of social exclusion, but also in many less visible form of resistance to building public housing in suburban or rural communities."[21]

Lindsey Hanley[22] talks about growing up in council estates as gradually building "brick by brick ... a wall in the head", borrowing the metaphor from '*die Mauer im Kopf*', a phase used to describe the attitude and feelings of residents of the former East and West Germany after the fall of the Berlin Wall, when they often acted as if a physical and institutional barrier was still there. The complex psychological relationship between the residents of former East and West Germany highlights how an imaginary barrier is erected through positive feedback loops between the perceived identity of a group, their own evolving identity, and institutional changes. Similarly, for UK council estates, the interplay of the complex issues around the identities of tenants, the perceptions of them from those outside the public housing system (including the media), and policies institutionalising an aspiration to own property, such as the right–to–buy, have created an immaterial but real barrier around those who live in them.

For Hanley, "being working class in Britain means to have a wall in the head, and since council housing has come to mean housing for the working class (and the non–working class) that wall exists unbroken throughout every estate in the land. The wall might be invisible, in that no one has built a fortress of bricks around every area of municipal housing, like ten thousand Cutteslowe Walls, but it's there, heavy and strong and as thickly invisible as Pyrex."[23]

By the end of the 1960s it was clear that council estate programmes could fail, and terms such as 'problem', 'difficult', 'difficult to let' or 'sink' began to be used to describe instances of estates that went wrong. Making sense of, and understanding the reasons for, the decline of estates, real or perceived, became an important aspect of academic debate. Studies to investigate reasons for this decline began to proliferate. These studies were attempting to address the same questions that had long troubled Victorian reformers, that is, whether the failure of housing estates is attributable to physical conditions and the design of the dwellings or to the 'defects of their inhabitants'. "That the question still needed to be asked at all perhaps showed how low the early idealism of council housing had fallen. The belief that slum people were a race apart had now all but receded into history, but, with underpinning from psychology, it was replaced by the notion of a small minority of 'problem tenants."[24]

A study of 'difficult' estates in Bristol categorised residents as 'solids', 'brittles' and 'difficults', and identified inception and any time when new populations are introduced as high–risk periods in an estate's lifetime.[25] The report concluded that 'difficult' estates, made difficult by disruptive minorities, are a "potentially permanent feature of the social landscape".[26] Similarly, a number of other studies placed an emphasis on the problems arising from re–housing. In the Newkirk Estate in Edinburgh, for instance, Harrington found that moving had damaged residents' sense of identity since "the old groups, of which they are a part, have broken up";[27]

on the Deneside Estate in Oldham, Shenton described a portion of deprived 'dissociates', part of a subculture to be found in most urban areas;[28] another study maintained that the root of problem estates were anti–social families who tended to 'gravitate' to those estates that already contain problem tenants "because, being of a like mind to others in the area, they find their behaviour accepted and even condoned"[29].

A turn in perspective was promoted by a seminal study at Moorepark in Govan, an area offensively dubbed 'Wine Alley' with a re–housing scheme perceived as 'difficult'. To conduct this study Damer[30] lived on the estate for nine months after which he concluded that the estate had been unfairly stigmatised and that the negative public perception was attributable to prejudice. An exploratory study by Building Research Establishment confirmed Wilson's conclusion that the most critical times for an estate are its inception and during 'invasions' by different populations; the study also identified some factors that appeared to distinguish problem estates: a high percentage of unskilled residents, wives not in paid employment, high child densities, high tenancy turnover.[31]

A deterministic view of tenant behaviour was promoted by Oscar Newman's study of New York's high–rise public estates, in which he introduced the concept of 'defensible space', based on a hypothesis that built environment physical features could promote either social or anti–social behaviour.[32] Newman's theory was validated in the UK context by a large–scale, somewhat controversial, study of London's high–rise and deck–access estates by Alice Coleman, which argued that size and other design features induced a general 'social malaise' indicated in elements such as crime, poverty, litter, graffiti, dog litter and numbers of children in care.[33] Coleman's 'environmental determinism' was hailed by the Conservative administration of the time, which implemented its recommendations in the Design Improvement Controlled Experiment (DICE). Newman and Coleman's ideas also laid the foundations for what would later become the 'secure by design' agenda, which prescribed design features such as easily monitored cul de sacs, 'target hardening'[34] and 'in–curtilage' parking. This approach contrasts starkly with established urban design principles of permeability, connectedness to social and spatial networks and the encouragement of activity as a deterrent for crime. The fundamental difference in approaches and underpinning ideology results in ongoing tensions between the 'grid' of urban designers and the 'enclave' supported by many residents, housing associations, local authorities and police.

There has been a shift in the discourse around the problems of social housing estates from being attributed to their size, their concentration of disadvantaged people and their stigmatisation and distinctiveness,[35] to a focus on social inclusion, mixed communities and sustainability[36]. Addressing social exclusion and inequalities translates not only into physically undifferentiated stock for all types of tenants and home owners, but also into measures to make housing more financially secure. Janet Ford argues that "security in housing matters because losing one's home can have devastating consequences including poverty, relationship breakdown, psychological distress, labour market and social exclusion, ill health, domestic violence, forced mobility and homelessness"[37]. Ford explores the issues that link financial insecurity with housing insecurity, highlights an increasing financial insecurity for both renters and home owners and warns about how, for tenants, issues related to Housing Benefit administration are a "critical factor in generating or amplifying financial insecurity".[38] At the time of writing, an immense threat to housing security is posed by the proposed housing reforms being unleashed by the Conservative–Liberal Democrat coalition. These reforms throw a double blow to housing security by proposing to end life–long council housing tenure, whilst, at the same time capping Housing Benefit.

Turning round

The failures and shortcomings of council estates resulting from the policies towards them perpetuated amongst certain groups have been highly visible and images of degradation, social problems, isolation and neglect are still strongly associated with them. Somehow they speak much louder than the thousands of tenants' testimonies that could be gathered to qualify the everyday in council estates in positive terms. While the failures seem to relate to the public and civic sphere, the positive experiences often pertain to the private sphere and are less visible, less memorable. Exceptions are those experiences that, often starting with acts of resistance and struggles, through inclusion empowerment, determination and, sometimes, serendipity, turned around what was deemed to be damned. One of these situations that resulted in positive change is that of Hulme, which went from worst slum in Manchester to what is widely considered one of the best examples of regeneration in Britain. A study by Moobela maps the regeneration processes between 1960 and 2002 against the characteristic features of an evolving organic system, producing a rich historical narrative of the relationship between local government and local communities in the context of decision-making around the development and the future of four huge crescent blocks of housing.[39] Hulme's narrative is articulated into episodes of protest and coming together, with positions of despair and openness, with progressive experimentation and actions and interventions at personal, collective and institutional levels from those involved. After years of uncertainty, demolition and reconstruction, the 70% of residents who chose to stay emerged to "a new-found dignity and security in homes they regarded as 'superior to most of the private housing that has been built'."[40]

Another example of a partnership amongst all stakeholders in a problem estate is that of the Manor in Sheffield. Following the collapse of the city's major manufacturing industries, coupled with changes in social policy towards a reduction of public expenditure in social services, Manor slipped into a rapid decline, going from being a relatively wealthy area to an estate whose community was largely unemployed. This economic decline was accelerated and exacerbated by the deterioration of the housing stock, and ultimately resulted in a social decline with a rise in crime, drop in levels of education achievements and poor health. In 1996, the Manor Estate was branded by *The Guardian* as the "worst estate in Britain". This labelling spurred local government into actively supporting residents' initiatives and activities, and the Manor and Castle Development Trust was formed as a partnership between community and the public and private sectors with a holistic and community–led approach to community regeneration. The trust was successful in attracting funding for an integrated system of complementary projects, from children's centres to a progressive green infrastructure strategy, and is transforming Manor Estate into an exemplar of sensitive and inclusive regeneration.

Resistance and protest have been identified above as being present in some of the episodes at the root of instances of changes in policies and successful estate regeneration. It could be argued that one particular form or tactic of resistance is self–organisation. "Contemporary urban space is, more than ever, determined by capitalist controlling logics of the market and of individualism. Under such logics, at the moments at which social and spatial conditions meet, there exist sites of both contestation and opportunity."[41] The formation of one self–organised group in a fertile context can sometimes create positive feedback loops and spur the emergence of a flurry of other self–organised groups. This emergence of bottom–up self–organised initiatives can, sometimes, be engineered or accelerated from the top–down through policies. One such case is the housing cooperative scene in Liverpool. The first housing coops, refurbishing existing stock, were formed in 1970 by small groups of working–class residents, with the support of the Shelter Neighbourhood Action Plan (SNAP), to create an alternative to the poor condition homes that they were living in[42] and in response to the threat of re–housing and dispersal. The Cooperative Development Service (CDS) was set up in 1976 as a housing association with a remit to encourage residents to become actively involved in the control and management of their homes and played an important role in catalysing the emergence of tenant–led coop initiatives. CDS supported a group of residents with the dream of designing, building and managing their homes to develop the Weller Street Housing Co–operative, the first new–build housing coop in the country, whose 'struggle' is captured in *The Weller Way*[43]. An interesting housing coop in Liverpool is the Eldonian Housing Cooperative, set up by a group of tenants from Eldon Rd who were "facing demolition of their neighbourhood and the destruction of their community"; the Eldonians designed and implemented an alternative strategy for the regeneration of their neighbourhood.[44]

At Coin Street in London's South Bank area, a local community organ-isation took it upon itself to provide alternative proposals to oppose a speculative office and hotel development. What initially seemed a hopeless and unjust battle, of a community against the forces of capitalism, turned into a thriving cluster of high quality housing cooperatives and social enterprises, seen by many as a footprint for community–led regeneration and housing provision. Affordability and accessibility are at the core of the Coin Street Housing Coops' ethos: the lease is owned by the Coin Street Community Builders (CSCB) and individual tenants have no right to own their homes; half of the tenants are nominated by the council and half are local tenants in 'housing need'. The longevity of the community living in the various Coin Street coops is supported by enabling all tenants to engage with the management of the coop and to adjust to a cooperative way of life: all new tenants are required to complete a course of 11 three–hour sessions covering how to run a cooperative, how to communicate with others and how to make collective decisions.[45] CSCB has enjoyed substantial growth in the past 20 years, largely thanks to the ownership of the land; whilst this growth can be seen as a reflection of the success of CSCB, it also carries the potential threat of undermining its founding principles.

What now?

The current economic crisis exposed the fragility of a social and affordable housing supply largely dependent, through Section 106, on private developers: lack of opportunities for high–margin profitable developments has meant a decline in the affordable housing provision. Critiques of the growth–based capitalist economic system are not new. In 1971 the Meadows Report[46] highlighted concerns about "the long–term causes and consequences of growth in population, industrial capital, food production, resource consumption, and pollution".[47] In the same year, Nicholas Georgescu–Roegen presented his bioeconomic programme, in which he argued that the sustainability of a sub–system needs to be assessed on the sustainability of the entire system that contains it, and facing the entropic limitations on the material output of the economic system, he emphasised the importance of the enjoyment of life as the real output of the economic process.[48] This emphasis on enjoyment of life has been become central to the French Decroissance[49] project, encapsulated in the strap–line of French magazine *La Decroissance: 'le journal de la joie de vivre'*, and is at the core of the growing field of happiness economics. Quality of life and 'happiness' as satisfaction of needs have been the driver for a number of projects and initiatives advocating, from the seventeenth, to various degrees, a just and equitable society, where resources are shared and fairly distributed and where self–interest is aligned with common purposes and collective benefit: from Levellers/Diggers and Plotlanders to Community Land Trusts, Cooperatives and Garden Cities. More recently the concomitance of environmental and financial crises created a push towards cooperative and mutual arrangements and projects based on ethical, mutual relationships amongst individuals and with the environment are gaining renewed strength: the Transition Towns movement, evolved from Permaculture, eco–villages rooted in model villages and garden cities experiences, co–housing and housing cooperatives are only some examples.

In recent years there has been a significant shift towards the social economy that has resulted in a political commitment, by both main parties, to supporting the growth of the Third Sector, giving communities the means to provide needed services in a way that best suits them. The rise and promotion of the Third Sector, while laudable and desirable in many ways, can also be seen to mask a withdrawal of the state from the provision of core services and duties. After the substantial cuts to the welfare system by the neo–liberal Conservatives (1979 to 1997) and the resulting significant increases in inequality and poverty, New Labour introduced a Third Way social policy; this policy has perhaps furthered the neo–liberalism programme more than it has reinstated welfare. Open support for the Third Sector is growing further under the Conservative–Liberal Democrat coalition, but behind the rhetoric of the 'Big Society' lies a cynical offloading of the responsibilities of the state.

With regards to housing, there is a very interesting emerging landscape made of cooperatives, co–housing schemes, mutual ownership schemes, user developed housing. A report by the New Economics Foundation, *Common Ground – For Mutual Ownership*, explores the scope of a housing model hinged on a "Community Land Trust, designed to extract the land from the market and retain it as a public asset, so that affordability is preserved on a long–term basis, and a co–operative form of tenure".[50] This model has since been refined, developed and publicised and there are now a handful of such schemes being explored.

Similar innovations and experiences are also emerging in Europe, where there is a much stronger cooperative tradition in housing. Particularly innovative is a proposal for a law put forward by the French Green Party (*Les Verts*) on 'third sector participatory ecological housing' that proposes the radical establishment of the right for communities to experiment and to be innovative with their housing provision.[51]

All these initiatives have the potential to deliver housing that is decoupled from the logic of capitalist growth, no longer a commodity, but simply a place to live, in a society that is more equal and just.[52] These housing models, however, are not substitutes for public housing provision: they can only complement it. Public provision of housing should be saved and safeguarded. Hills' study on the future of social housing in England stresses the importance of looking after the existing stock and of current tenants compared with newly built stock and incoming tenants: "It seems likely, even if there were a sustained increase in the rate of building new social housing, for instance, that we already have 90 per cent of the stock we will have in ten years' time. Yet the focus of policy and of the policy debate is often overwhelmingly on the new stock and on access routes to social housing. This seems unbalanced, not just because it means that too little attention may be being given to the needs and lives of the nearly four million households already living in social housing, but also because mistakes in managing and looking after the existing stock can entirely offset the benefits of getting things right on the new supply". Hills also stresses how mistakes such as failure to maintain stock adequately and to prevent decline in neighbourhood conditions, or to keep an income mix that would avoid stigmatisation would "offset more than a year's new production".[53]

Estates should have access to adequate resources and support in a long–term view where the cost of upgrading and maintaining as well as managing the stock is offset by social benefits of thriving housing communities. Even in a cost cutting, shrinking, pure accounting logic, the social return on investment of a well functioning social housing system should make a convincing case for investing in its upkeep (if short–termism is put aside, that is). All attempts to unravel public housing should be seen as politics.

*The author would like to thank the agency research group for providing an inspiring environment. Tatjana Schneider for her relentless generosity. Studio 8 [Housing +] students (2008-09 and 2009-10) for creating a stimulating forum for exploring and challenging housing production. Mark Parsons for his patience and his help on every level.

1. A. Ravetz, *Council Housing and Culture* (London: Routledge, 2001) p. 5.
2. *ibid.*, Ravetz (2001) p. 2.
3. C. Holmes, *A New Vision for Housing* (London: Routledge, 2005) p. 198.

4. The First World War indirectly provided an impetus in housing policy as the poor physical health and fitness of many army recruits from urban areas became apparent and acknowledged. This led to the Tudor Walters Committee being set up, the Homes Fit for Heroes Campaign, and the Addison Act (1919).
5. In 1911 the resistance of the poorly housed started when the Admiralty torpedo workers rejected tenement houses offered to them in Greenock (D. Whitham, 'The First Sixty Years of Council Housing' in J. English (ed.) *Future of Council Housing*, Croom Helm, 1982) and built up to cause what Swenarton calls 'Bolshevism and Revolution', a lecture by Lloyd George to his cabinet in 1919(M. Swenarton, *Homes Fit for Heroes*, Farnham: Ashgate, 1981).
6. *ibid.*, Holmes (2005) p. 12.
7. B. Franklin, *Housing Transformations* (London: Routledge, 2006) p. 52.
8. I. Cole & R. Furbey, *The Eclipse of Council Housing* (London: Routledge, 1993).
9. A total of 156,000 prefabricated houses were provided; these houses proved very popular and generally outlived their life expectancy.
10. P. Dunleavy, *The Politics of Mass Housing in Britain, 1945–75: Study of Corporate Power and Professional Influence in the Welfare State* (Oxford: Oxford University Press, 1981).
11. Dept. of Environment, *Homes for Today and Tomorrow* (London: Stationery Office Books, 1961).
12. A. Ravetz, *Remaking Cities* (London: Croom Helm, 1980).
13. *ibid.*, Franklin (2006) p. 53.
14. *ibid.*, Holmes (2005) p. 56.
15. *ibid.*, Holmes (2005) p. 58.
16. H. Pawson & C. Fancy, *Maturing Assets: The Evolution of Stock Transfer Housing Associations* (Bristol: Policy Press, 2003).
17. *ibid.*, Holmes (2005) p. 64.
18. L. Hanley, *Estates: An Intimate History* (London: Granta Books, 2008) p. 20.
19. J. Dean & A. Hastings, *Challenging Images: Housing Estates, Stigma and Regeneration* (Bristol: Policy Press, 2000).
20. *ibid.*, Dean & Hastings (2000) p. 27.
21. *ibid.*, Holmes (2005) p. 194.
22. *ibid.*, Hanley (2008).
23. *ibid.*, Hanley (2008) p. 149.
24. *ibid.*, Ravetz (2001) p. 183.
25. R. Wilson, *Difficult housing estates* (London: Tavistock Publications, 1963).
26. *ibid.*, Wilson (1963) p. 22.
27. Molly Harrington, 'Resettlement and Self–image', *Human Relations*, 1965, 18:115, p. 136.
28. Neil Shenton, Deneside – *A Council Estate*, York: University of York, 1976).
29. *Difficult to Let Estates – Report of a Study Group* (Gateshead: Northern Consortium of Housing Authorities, 1981), http://opensigle.inist.fr/handle/10068/554615.
30. S. Damer, 'Wine Alley: the sociology of a dreadful enclosure', *Sociological Review*, 22 (2) pp. 221–48.
31. J.J. Attenburrow, A.R. Murphy & A.G. Simms, *The Problems of Some Large Local Authority Estates – an exploratory study* (London: HMSO, 1978).
32. O. Newman, *Defensible Space; Crime Prevention Through Urban Design* (London: Macmillan, 1973).
33. A.M. Coleman, *Utopia on Trial: Vision and Reality in Planned Housing* (London: Hilary Shipman Ltd., 1985).

34. Target hardening is a term referring to the strengthening of the security of a building in order to reduce or minimise the risk of attack or theft based on the assumption that a visible defence will deter or delay an attack. In the context of housing, target hardening may also be referred to as crime prevention through environmental design. This can include ensuring all doors and windows are closed and securely locked, removing any trees or bushes that could offer suitable hiding places or could be used to climb to a higher level of the property.
35. *ibid.*, Franklin (2006) p. 98.
36. P. Somerville, 'Explanations of Social Exclusion: Where Does Housing Fit in?', *Housing Studies*, 1998, 13(6), p. 761; John Hills, *Ends and Means: The future roles of social housing in England* (London: Centre for Analysis of Social Exclusion, LSE, 2007) available at: http://sticerd.lse.ac.uk/dps/case/cr/CASEreport34.pdf; J. Ford, 'Staying Put? Secure and Insecure Housing', D. Dorling et al., The Great Divide: *An Analysis of Housing Inequality* (London: Shelter, 2005).
37. *ibid.*, Ford (2005) p. 144.
38. *ibid.*, Ford (2005) p. 144.
39. Cletus Moobela, 'From worst slum to best example of regeneration: complexity in the regeneration of Hulme, Manchester', *International Journal of Emergence, Coherence and Organisations* (E:CO), 2005, 7(1), pp. 29–42.
40. Rob Ramwell & Hilary Saltburn, *Trick or Treat? City Challenge and the Regeneration of Hulme* (York: North British Housing Association and Guinness Trust, 1998) p. 83, cited in ibid., Ravetz (2001) p. 234.
41. S. Vardy, 'Spatial Agency: Tactics of Self–Organisation', *Architectural Research Quarterly*, 2009, 13(02), pp. 133–140.
42. *ibid.*, Holmes (2005) p. 162.
43. A. McDonald, *The Weller Way: The Story of the Weller Street Housing Cooperative* (London: Faber, 1986).
44. J. McBane, *The Rebirth of Liverpool: The Eldonian Way* (Liverpool: Liverpool University Press, 2008).
45. *ibid.*, Holmes (2005) p. 166.
46. D. Meadows, *Limits to Growth: A Report for the Club of Rome's Project on the Predicament of Mankind* (Earth Island, 1972), available at: http://www.context.org/ICLIB/IC32/Meadows.htm (accessed 23/04/10).
47. A new update to *The Limits to Growth* reveals that we are closer to "overshoot and collapse" – yet sustainability is still an achievable goal. Donella H. Meadows, Dennis L. Meadows & Jørgen Randers, 'Beyond The Limits To Growth', *In Context, a Quarterly Of Humane Sustainable Culture: Dancing Toward The Future*, 1992, 32, available at: http://www.context.org/ICLIB/IC32/Meadows.htm (accessed 23/04/10).
48. N. Georgescu–Roegen, *The Entropy Law and the Economic Process* (Cambridge, MA: Harvard University Press, 1971).
49. Degrowth.
50. Pat Conaty et al., *Common Ground – for Mutual Home Ownership Community land trusts and shared–equity co–operatives to secure permanently affordable homes for key workers* (London: New Economics Foundation and CDS Co–operatives, 2003).
51. Noël Mamère, *De la reconnaissance du statut de l'habitat participatif, diversifié et écologique (n° 1990)* (Paris: Assemblée nationale de France, 2009) available at: http://www.assemblee–nationale.fr/13/rapports/r2088.asp#P289_57648.
52. C. Cerulli, 'Housing with Joie de Vivre: Mutual Production Models for Sustainable Futures', in *Green Economics and Green Jobs* (Oxford: Green Economics Institute, 2010) pp. 54–60.
53. *ibid.*, Hills (2007) p. 169.

Biographies

Andrea Luka Zimmerman explores, though filmmaking, text and photo-graphy, the grey zones between public and private memory. Her practice aims to intervene in and rebel against the production of history and violence and to engage with everyday life within these systems. She was a founding member of Vision Machine (2001) which made, influenced by the methodology and thoughts of Jean Rouch, Miles Horton and Paolo Freire, *The Globalisation Tapes,* numerous shorter experimental films and gallery works as well as interventions in public space. She is currently (2010) completing her first feature length documentary, which is about a special forces commander that inspired the Rambo films. As Fugitive Images, Andrea collaborated with Lasse and Tristan on making the public art work *i am here,* installed on the facade of Samuel House on the Haggerston Estate.

Lasse Johansson works with film, photography and installation. Since graduating from Chelsea College of Art in 2001 he has explored issues around the formation of public spaces and the identities they give rise to. In 2002 he co–curated the public art exhibition *Contemplation Room* at Gallery Overgaden, in Copenhagen, together with Cecilie Gravesen and Kristine Agergaard. He has developed a prototype vertical garden to be used as a social sculpture on inner–city estates with no access to cultivatable land. In 2008 he completed an MA in Photography and Urban Culture at Goldsmiths College. His most recent works include the short film *Bruce & I* and the public art installation *i am here,* which he made in collaboration with Andrea and Tristan as Fugitive Images. He is currently collaborating with Andrea developing a film about Haggerston West & Kingsland Estates, which is part of their ongoing estate project.

Tristan Fennelll works with photography and installation to explore the conflict and collusion between individuals and the surrounding urban landscapes. Tristan is part of the artist collaboration, Fugitive Images, and with Andrea and Lasse made *i am here*. He graduated with an MA in Photography and Urban Culture from Goldsmiths College in 2007. His work has been exhibited at the Singapore International Photography Festival 2008, Les Rencontres d'Arles 2009 and the East London Photography Festival 2009.

Paul Hallam has written or co-written many screenplays including *A Kind of English* (Ruhul Amin), *Caught Looking* (Constantine Giannaris), *Nighthawks* (Ron Peck/Paul Hallam), *Strip Jack Naked* (Ron Peck) and *Young Soul Rebels* (Isaac Julien). His play, *The Dish*, was performed in London, New York and Toronto and adapted for a BBC Radio 4 broadcast; his first book, *The Book of Sodom*, is published by Verso; his *Briefplays* have appeared in performance, video and publication; and he has also published many essays. Three biographical/autobiographical films, *Soho* (Ron Peck/Paul Hallam), *King's Cross* (Kate Boyd/Paul Hallam) and *The Last Biscuit* (Paul Hallam/Andrea Luka Zimmerman) have recently been released on DVD. He lives in Istanbul where he is currently (2010) working on a book and film project, *The Turkish Dormitory*.

Victor Buchli is Reader in Material Culture in the Department of Anthropology and teaches on the Urban Studies Msc at University College London. His interests include architecture, domesticity, the archaeology of the recent past, critical understandings of materiality and new technologies and the anthropology of sustainability and design. He is a member of the Eco-Town Delivery Consortium through which he is conducting a long-term ethnographic project 'Assembling the Carbon Neutral Subject' and supervising research into the anthropology of ecologically sustainable development and design. Victor's publications include *An Archaeology of*

Socialism (Berg 1999), *Archaeologies of the Contemporary Past* (Routledge 2001, with Gavin Lucas) and *Interpreting Archaeology* (Routledge 1995, co-edited with Ian Hodder et al). He edited *The Material Culture Reader* (Berg 2002), *Material Culture: Critical Concepts in the Social Sciences* (Routledge 2004) and *Urban Life in Post Soviet Asia* (Routledge 2007, with C. Alexander and C. Humphrey), has been managing editor of the *Journal of Material Culture,* and is founding and managing editor of *HomeCultures.* He is working on a book on immateriality and another entitled *The Anthropology of Architecture* (Berg 2011).

Cristina Cerulli qualified as an *architetto* in Florence in 1999 and has worked in practice and academia. At the School of Architecture, University of Sheffield, since 2004, she teaches in the Master of Architecture and Master of Urban Design programmes and is active in research. She has been co-running, with Tatjana Schneider, a design studio looking at housing design from a social, economic and political perspective; her research interests range from community-led housing development models and shared models of living to alternative and creative forms of management and procurement, green economics, emergence, resilience and mutuality and collaboration. Cristina is also an active member of the research centre *agency: transformative research into practice and education.* She founded Studio Polpo with Mark Parsons in 2008.

Acknowledgements

We experienced a long journey with our many fellow residents at Haggerston West & Kingsland Estates and we would like to begin by acknowledging their contribution to this book. *Estate* brings together the stories, experiences, ideas and spaces of many residents. Such was their diversity, we could scarcely believe that all emerged from the same location.

A special thanks to Cristina Cerulli and Victor Buchli for their critical insights; and to Paul Hallam for developing the ideas driving this project with us.

We would like to thank Deepa Naik and Trenton Oldfield of Myrdle Court Press for working with us to define what now has become *Estate*. Karolin Schnoor brought together a vast visual archive with clarity and sensitivity and Barbara Murray kept our English on track.

Arts Council England saw the value of supporting an interdisciplinary publication between creative and academic practices that explores the processes, politics and experiences of public housing in the UK.

Hackney Council gave us access to the empty flats. London & Quadrant Housing Association gave further access and we thank them for allowing a critical debate about the complex process of regeneration and housing provision .PRP architects provided us with the original and future plans for Haggerston West & Kingsland Estates ; and the London School of Economics permitted the reproduction of the "Booth Map".

We would also like to thank a few individuals for their generous feedback, Bernard Walsh, Karen Mirza, Brad Butler, Basak Ertur, Nick Strauss, Neal Purvis, Lockheart Murdoch, Adam Clitheroe, Erol Kagan, Eleanor John, Tessa Garland and in particular Leighton Tervit, whose invaluable support from the start allowed us to go all the way.

We would finally take the opportunity to thank Rachel Baker, Claire McDonald, Manu Luksch, Mukul Patel, Gabriel Stubbs, Michael Holman, Sandra Collins, Maria Zeb Benjamin and Gesche Würfel who, at various stages, helped and encouraged us to realise the project.

73
64
6

fig.54